CHANEL
and her world

by Edmonde Charles-Roux

Weidenfeld & Nicolson

This book is dedicated
to the dual memory
of Michel de Brunhoff,
Editor-in-Chief of
the French edition of *Vogue,*
and of his son
Pascal de Brunhoff,
Parisian student who
in his twentieth year
was shot by the Nazis.

Translated from the French by Daniel Wheeler
Designed by Jackie Bouthillier
Picture Research by Dominique Paulve

© 1979 Sté Nlle des Éditions du Chêne
English translation © 1981 Hachette-Vendome

First published in Great Britain in 1981 by Weidenfeld and Nicolson,
91 Clapham High Street, London SW4

First paperback edition published 1982

ISBN 0 297 78195 2
Printed and bound in Italy by
Grafiche Editoriali Ambrosiani SpA, Milan

introduction

Chanel, who always seemed so utterly of our time, actually came from another century, having been born in 1883. In that year, President Chester Alan Arthur inaugurated a work of engineering then regarded as the ultimate in daring, the Brooklyn Bridge; in Moscow, Tsar Alexander II and his Tsaritsa, more bedecked than idols (she under some 32 kilos of silver fabric), were crowned Emperor and Empress of all the Russias; in Paris, news arrived that the French flag had just been raised over the citadel of Hanoi; in Berlin, vindictive articles, signed by Bismarck, proclaimed that France was decidedly a nation of madmen; and in London, the subjects of austere Queen Victoria asked themselves whether Her Majesty could have been in love with her man-servant? Deeply affected by the death of John Brown, the elderly monarch canceled all audiences. No newspaper, however, made note of the fact that in a hospital deep within provincial France a second child had been born to a poor, unmarried couple. The father was a small-wares peddler from the Cévennes, the mother a peasant of stock native to Auvergne, and the newborn a little girl named Gabrielle Chanel. In her own way, she too would reign, rule, and govern.

Why was it that, having completely escaped the absurdities of the fashion world, Mademoiselle Chanel would to the end of her days strive relentlessly to conceal her personal origins? The father of Chanel, if one believed what she said, was a man of mystery, who fathered more children than he could feed, spent more than he earned, and finally disappeared. But how did he make a living? To this question Chanel never gave a reply. We shall never know why Gabrielle Chanel adopted such reticence in regard to her family—her several brothers, her mother whose early death left little Gabrielle to the mercies of a provincial orphanage.

The story of Chanel is difficult to tell. She did not even experience what most women of her generation did—marriage and children. Abandoned by her father the week after her mother died, Gabrielle the child suffered all the harshness of convent life, by which we do not mean misery and maltreatment but, rather, strictness, solitude, and mental anguish.

Then came problematic beginnings.

What could be hoped, at that time, for a poor girl brought up by the charity of nuns? Gabriel risked, while barely out of adolescence, finding herself placed as a clerk with some regional tradesman. This was what she must resist, what she must escape. Already at age eighteen, she had no other thought. Still, the young Chanel made her start in Moulins with just such an employment, working under a shopkeeper specializing in layettes, linens, and small wares.

Several years passed, filled mainly with false starts. Among these was a move to Vichy, where, dreaming of a career in the theatre, she made a stab at singing and even dancing.

Chanel was twenty-five when she met the scion of a high bourgeois family, who proposed, not marriage, but a life together. This was Étienne Balsan, a gentleman horse breeder and riding enthusiast. Chanel accepted and moved in with him near Paris. Now began an apprenticeship that would reveal to her both the charms of château life and the secrets of the role that had devolved upon her: She was succeeding the celebrated courtesan Émilienne d'Alençon as the *châtelain's* official mistress.

One can imagine the exasperation of Gabrielle Chanel in later years whenever she read the legends that had her leaving her native province attired in a cotton apron and *sabots*. No doubt she was put together in a simple manner, but it is certain that upon her arrival in Paris in 1909, Chanel was already dressed according to her own taste—that is, like no one else—and possessed of that vibrant inner quality which would make her unforgettable to everyone she met.

Now commenced a whimsical period during which Chanel drank deeply of whatever the cup of life offered. She became both equestrienne and seductress, exercizing the best horses then available in France and exploiting the assets that were peculiarly her own: great natural beauty and a rare charm. Seen everywhere—Paris, Pau, Cannes, Deauville—Chanel emerged as the darling of all the young lions of the age. After Balsan came "Boy" Capel, a brilliantly intelligent Englishman and her greatest—possibly her only—love. But he too merely made Chanel his mistress, without there ever being the possibility of marriage.

Happy? Gabrielle Chanel pretended that she was, although many years later she would admit, in rare, unguarded moments, that this was a time, more than ever afterwards, when she often found herself in tears. She also professed to have had only modest aspirations, wanting true love, to be chosen, preferred, and that the choice be for always. But destiny decreed that such happiness would never be hers.

In the summer of 1913 Chanel decided to break with the life of a kept woman and all the vexations it entailed. Thus, with the financial help of Boy Capel, she settled in Deauville and opened her first boutique. She entered into the affair with drums beating, as if, by the weight of her own body, she were forcing open the door to freedom.

Nothing thereafter would make Chanel give up an activity that, however much it may have originated as merely a means of taking revenge upon life, soon became her whole *raison d'être*. And nothing could stop her, not even the war that exploded within a year, nor yet the rumble of cannons sounding all the way from Verdun. Once she began to apply herself, Chanel became a *femme d'entreprise* forever. Throughout the remainder of her life she would work unremittingly as both craftsman and businesswoman, imposing her personal conception of the art of dressing upon an ever-expanding clientele. Along the way she crossed swords with the greatest *couturier* of the age, Paul Poiret, taking his customers one by one and recruiting them into the band of women who, on her orders, gave up aigrettes, long hair, and hobble skirts.

In the postwar era, beginning in 1918, and then again in the prewar period of the thirties, Chanel received the attentions of high-born, aristocratic suitors. The first was the extraordinarily handsome, but ruined and exiled, Grand Duke Dmitri of Russia, the second the fabulously rich and powerful Duke of Westminster. In her own way, Chanel derived real benefit from these liaisons. With the Russian she developed a taste for warm, fur-lined coats and for fabrics of almost Byzantine opulence, while through the Englishman she fell in love with British tweeds, which she had women wear with jersey blouses and ropes of pearls, a revolutionary combination at the time. She also acquired the English respect for comfort, and never again allowed that luxury could have any purpose other than to make simplicity appear remarkable.

Chanel never resisted the association of her name with those of the two aristocrats, which, however, cannot be construed to mean that these were the men to whom she felt the most attached. Her heart concealed other memories, other, long-lost loves, other sorrows, and once she had determined that a name should not be mentioned, never again would a syllable of it pass her lips.

Then came another war and the French defeat. In occupied Paris the sound of German boots made the benign fashion parade over which Chanel presided seem totally futile. Thus, she demobilized her battalion of mannequins and the next morning closed the House of Chanel. For this action Chanel suffered the most severe criticism, with the fashion industry accusing her of desertion. She could not have cared less.

The Occupation proved to be a dark moment in the life of Chanel. Her affair with a German officer, although discreetly conducted, created a scandal as soon as it was known and then brought violent recriminations once the war was over.

Peace returned, but prewar France had ceased to exist. No one was more conscious of this than Gabrielle Chanel. Where, for instance, were the millionaires of old? The foreign women who formerly came to Paris and bought dresses by the dozen? Chanel did not reopen her salon. Withdrawn into herself and self-exiled to Switzerland, she watched with peasant shrewdness and kept quiet. This inactivity continued for a full decade.

Paris quickly forgets. Soon no one spoke of Chanel, and a new public knew her merely as a name. As for Chanel, only the rising star of a very great *couturier* could revive the old sense of competition. But Christian Dior at his zenith promised to be a worthy adversary. In 1954 Chanel set out to destroy him as if it were a holy mission. In this she did not succeed, but she managed, in her lightning reappearance, to challenge him quite seriously. Indeed, Chanel realized a new and immense success. Thus did this indomitable woman, now seventy-one years old, rediscover the old passion for her *métier*. She worked with a ferocious dedication—as well as with utter indifference to the emotional disarray caused by her demands and rages. Whenever these rang out, the life of a building with several stories and a staff of hundreds remained suspended as if from her fingers or from the very sound of her voice.

It was something to live with Chanel those days and nights prior to the first showing of each new collection. And to see her exhausted, having consumed nothing since morning but a glass of water, yet still hard at it because forever unsatisfied. So exalted was her idea of perfection that she could tolerate none of the compromises that are the stock-in-trade of others. It was also something to hear "Mademoiselle," her mouth full of invective, launch into one of the soliloquies that with her passed for conversation and that accompanied her battle with thread, wool, fabric, the difficult shape, or anything else that resisted her.

How many nights, how many days did Chanel spend in this way during her long life? Was it really necessary to go to such lengths in order to be, in the eyes of the world, the great Chanel?

Chanel lived at the very center of an extraordinary professional success, yet she suffered extreme loneliness, having failed in what meant the most to her—the life of a woman. What she had, however, was more independence, more freedom than most could ever imagine.

Her fate stands in contradiction to the thesis that equality between the sexes is the determining condition of female happiness. As a business executive, Chanel proved to be altogether the equal of men, often their superior, but in her private life she was the most vulnerable of women. The worst of it was that while fashion may have constituted the focus of her entire existence, this grand preoccupation could not satisfy her need for love, a realm in which Gabrielle Chanel met nothing but disillusionment.

Occasionally, at the end of her strength, Chanel could be heard saying to herself: "Ah! I shall die of it." One's heart went out to her. After all, to die for an armhole, for a braid positioned a bit higher or lower, to perish for a certain idea of elegance—did this not take it a bit too far? But the battle went on and on, as long as Chanel had breath.

It was at the end of a week in which she may have thought more often than usual, "Ah! I shall die of it," that Gabrielle Chanel breathed no more. The 10th of June 1971 fell on Sunday, the day of rest. When her heart stopped, the great woman was eighty-seven years old. Her reign over the world of fashion had endured almost half a century.

Edmonde Charles-Roux

in the chestnut groves of the Cévennes

This hamlet in the Cévennes was the geographic cradle of the Chanel family. But not even in her most candid and confidential moments would Gabrielle Chanel, that otherwise courageous and liberated woman, ever have admitted that her ancestors came from Ponteils. Like all the inhabitants of the hamlet, the Chanels were originally rural folk with scarcely any land, hiring out to gather chestnuts and living almost exclusively by this means—well or badly depending on the harvest. At the beginning of the 19th century the great-grandfather of Gabrielle made a marriage that permitted him to give up day labor and stop breaking his back for others. Using his wife's very modest dowry, he rented a hall and there opened a tavern. Today the local people still say *le Chanel* in referring to the farmhouse that once sheltered the country bistro of Ponteils.

1 Harvesting chestnuts with large tongs.
2 Ponteils today, with its great chestnut tree and what remains of *le Chanel*.
3 With no one to harvest them, the chestnuts of Ponteils lie strewn over the ground.

Over a century and a half have passed since the great-grandfather of Gabrielle Chanel served as tavern keeper in this simple, primitive, and virtually unchanged Cévenole farmhouse, using as his public room an outbuilding space rented from a small landholder. The appearance of a village café marked the true turning point in the mores of the rural world. By relieving isolation, it also ruptured the unity of family life, while affecting many other traditions and customs, such as evenings at home before the fire. Now the men who remained in Ponteils gathered every night in the bistro. But even these were old men, for the city had claimed the younger ones. Such was the general trend during the 1850–80 period, and the descendants of tavern keeper Chanel were no exception. Both his son and his grandson became itinerant peddlers, and both fathered children by women they had not married. It was to the younger couple—to the *mercelot* father—that Gabrielle Chanel was born in 1883. Ponteils, a bastion of the peasant spirit, really discloses the most about the bold and indomitable *couturière*.

1 A wasted plant—all that remains of the arbor.
2 A "beehive" house with the ground floor used for sheltering carriages, equipment, and animals.
3 An arch leads to the cellar of this economical and carefully organized dwelling, a functional farmhouse providing a good volume of enclosed space for all the necessities of daily life.
4 A fortress-like house that one day had to be abandoned.
5 The peasants have gone, leaving everything as it was.
6 The "common" or family room so essential to peasant life. Its "décor" is typical of taverns during the period when rural France went into decline with the flight of the peasantry to the city.

in Saumur it was still Second Empire

Saumur, a city simultaneously gay and strict, severe and roistering, was totally devoted to horsemanship. Masters and students at the cavalry school reigned over an equestrian city that lived for them. The French defeat of 1870–71, the arrival of the Prussians in Paris, the abdication of Napoleon III, the burning of the Tuileries—all this had occurred less than thirteen years before the birth of Gabrielle Chanel in 1883. The Empire was only yesterday, but the fashions of that era had already disappeared from the street. Among the cavalrymen, uniforms were now more severe, with a low *képi* replacing the tall *shako* as headgear. Still, there remained the frogs and loops, the passementerie braids, and on jackets (oh Chanel!) nine gold buttons, the privilege of the military.

1   Saumur at the end of the 19th century. The horsemen of the Cadre Noir report to the Manège ("Riding Academy"), their gold-banded whips held like scepters. Along the way ladies are honored with devouring glances.
2   Late-19th-century engraving. Lovely evenings in Saumur. The second lieutenants enjoy their street encounters with the *cocottes avec equipage.*
3   Feminine conquest, a sport like any other.
4   19th-century engraving. The women called "little allies" were not ruinous mistresses. A dinner here, a hat there—this was about all the young bucks of Saumur had to offer, leaving the street girls to live and die in poverty.

August in Saumur

This was the month of the Carrousel, the event of the year, the festival of festivals. That day the entire school could be found on the Chardonnet, the field where everything happened—quadrilles, reviews, the presentation of troops, riding instructions. On August 19, 1883, the female companion of a small-wares peddler hurried across the merry town, a lone figure directing her steps toward the hospital. There Jeanne Devolle gave birth to Gabrielle.

1   The word *hospice* was inscribed across the austere portal that guarded access to what once was a lazar-house administered by the Order of Saint John. To give birth in this "hospital" was considered by bourgeois women to reflect an almost shameful poverty.
2   A Carrousel day with officers, noncoms, and their instructors. Here too some foreign students, mainly Russians who one day would serve in the horseguard of Tsar Nicholas II.

the birth of Gabrielle Chanel

On August 20, 1883, Gabrielle was taken to the townhall by three employees of the hospital. They registered her as the child of Albert Chanel, merchant, and a shop girl named Devolle, domiciled "with her husband." The latter was absent. No one knew the exact spelling of Chanel, and so the mayor improvised, adding an "s" to the infant's paternal name. The three members of the hospital staff were all illiterate. Consequently, an age-old formula had to be used: "Having said they did not know how to read, did not sign the present document, which was read aloud." The mayor then signed what otherwise would have been a virtually anonymous paper.

3 In the hospital chapel where, on August 21, Gabrielle was baptized hangs an important painting by Philippe de Champaigne: *Simeon Receiving the Infant Jesus at the Entrance to the Temple* (detail of Mary and Joseph).

4 The birth certificate of Gabrielle Chanel, 1883.

life in the public markets

In 1884 the mother of Gabrielle was offered what she had long despaired of: marriage to Albert Chanel, with whom she had been living for three years. In the margin of the marriage certificate appear the names of two children—Julia and Gabrielle—whom Albert recognized as his. Together—he very much the cock of the village walk, she sweet and submissive—they brought up their daughters in the public markets. Very few French cities provided covered markets in those days. Fairs, religious festivals, peasant gatherings involving entire families—all took place out-of-doors, with merchants and merchandise alike exposed to every kind of weather. It was in this humble world that Gabrielle spent her childhood. The greatest problem for itinerant merchants was to find a city to work out from. For two years Albert made Issoire the point of departure for his peregrinations. From the small-wares peddler that he

was, Albert Chanel evolved into a sort of traveling salesman specializing in workclothes and undergarments.

1 *Marchandes au panier, crieuses, marchandes des quatre-saisons*—subtle differences distinguished the types of work available to women in the markets.

2 Note the marked contrast between the rich attire of the woman wearing a hat and the peasant dress of the *marchande*.

3 All the wretchedness of the late 19th century is expressed in the faces and forms of these women seated on a curbstone offering their pitiful wares.

4 By the end of the 19th century small country markets like this one were threatened by the lure of the city—the metropolis that consumed, perverted, and depopulated rural France.

the abbey for orphan girls

Orphanage. If there was a word that never crossed the lips of Gabrielle Chanel, it was this one. She worked relentlessly to eradicate all traces of the unhappy fate that had been hers. When her mother died in 1895 Gabrielle was twelve years old. After a move from Brive to Aubazine, Albert Chanel abandoned his daughters to the region's largest orphanage.

1   Aerial view of the convent buildings and the wonderful abbey, so typical in plan of 12th-century Cistercian churches.
2   Situated upon a small plateau between the Corrèze and Coiroux valleys, the abbey nestles in a green and leafy world.
3   The vast halls, vaulted corridors, and echoing stairways of this monastic building once swarmed with black-clad orphan girls, whose sad existence Gabrielle and her sisters shared for six years.

Moulins,
city of Masses and processions

In 1900 Gabrielle had to make a choice. The Aubazine convent kept no orphans beyond age eighteen, except those wishing to enter the novitiate. Gabrielle was thus taken in by an institution in Moulins administered by a congregation of canonesses. There the occasions to go out were few, and the reason for them always had to be religious.

4 The kiosk where the local band, *La Lyre Moulinoise,* could be heard. This, one said, was no place for convent girls, but Gabrielle longed to attend the concerts.

5 High Masses out-of-doors and slow processions unfolded in Moulins with more ceremony, it seemed, than anywhere else in France.

6 Dressed alike, even to their straw hats, and flanked by priests in immaculate surplices, the handsome boys of Moulins were the city's principal Sunday attraction.

everything distinguished *demoiselles* from charity cases

In addition to paying students, the boarding school that took in Gabrielle Chanel and her sisters admitted free of charge, as did many such institutions of the time, a certain number of young women without means. On one side of the school were the young ladies who obviously enjoyed material advantages and, on the other, the poor girls. It was in the latter category that the canonesses enrolled Gabrielle. Almost nineteen upon arrival, she remained two years, treated always like an orphan on charity. Never once did her father give any sign of life.

1　Young women of a private boarding school at Moulins in 1895, all dressed in garnet-colored cashmere furnished by their families. The double wardrobe (for winter and summer) was both large and fine, consisting of "cap, straw boater, two dresses, two *pèlerines*, two cloaks, and two pairs of shoes *at least*."

2　The girls of the free school also wore *pèlerines*, but these were made of rough wool and knitted in the convent's workroom. The second-hand ankle boots were, like everything else, provided by the congregation.

3　During fairs, dog shearers served as coiffeurs. This made it possible to sell the tresses of penniless girls for a good price to ladies desiring additional hair, as well as to institutions teaching young women the art of embroidering with hair.

4　At a public fair, pretty little girls dressed in white pleats and lace collars crowd around the carousel.

5　No holiday hat for this charity pupil who, in cap and black smock, used her handkerchief to make a necktie.

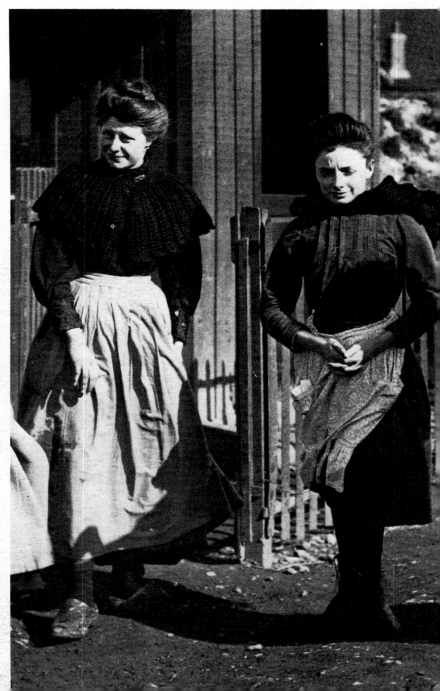

3

4

Fête des Cours 1910

5

A SAINTE-MARIE

SOIERIES — DENTELLES — RUBANS

Ancienne Maison GRAMPAYRE

H. DESBOUTIN-SOL

SUCCESSEUR

1, Rue de l'Horloge et 40, Rue d'Allier

MOULINS

Voilettes, Jupons, Broderies, Crêpes Anglais
Boas, Fourrures pour Dames, etc.

Doublures, Fournitures pour Couturières

Chanel, shop girl

A peasant insistence upon making a clear separation between workclothes and Sunday dress—the one functional, the other for show—and the conviction of people bound to the soil that only that which cannot be worn out should be used—all this Gabrielle Chanel had in her blood. When she was twenty, the canonesses placed her as a clerk in a thriving hosiery shop in Moulins run by some extremely decent folk.

near Sainte-Marie's

1 The sign proclaiming *Maison de Confiance*, fixed on the top frieze, proves that honesty was what sold best in provincial France.

2 Poster made c. 1910. A pious name—*À Sainte-Marie*—also inspired confidence. This was where Chanel had her first job, working as a shop clerk.

3 1909 photo. The Coutelard garage figured large in the sporting life of Moulins.

4 A commercial street in Moulins at the turn of the century.

5 At the intersection of the Rue de l'Horloge and the Rue d'Allier, the sign of the shop where Gabrielle Chanel and her Aunt Adrienne worked.

those gentlemen
of the 10th Chasseurs

Moulins could boast an important garrison. It billeted several regiments, but only one unit—and only from 1889 to 1913—really counted: the 10th Chasseurs, an aristocratic regiment and the ultra-smart club for sons of old families. The apprentice of the Rue de l'Horloge quickly became the toast of the young lieutenants. With Gabrielle's permission, these gallants made themselves her true discoverers. But the gentleman she came to prefer, the one who first loved her, was a young infantry officer whose family belonged to the Moulins district: Étienne Balsan, scion of the *haute bourgeoisie* and beneficiary of a considerable private income.

1   Gabrielle Chanel in 1903, when she was a shop girl in Moulins. With her, an officer of the 10th Chasseurs and one of her many admirers.
2   Étienne Balsan during his tour of duty with the 90th Infantry Regiment.
3   Moulins' Villars quarter billet of the Chasseurs, constructed during the reign of Louis-Philippe (1830–48).

debuts
at La Rotonde

The pavilion in Moulins known as La Rotonde was built around 1860 as a reading room, but barely three years later, as the *café-concert* rage spread throughout France, it became the setting for the region's best-known *concert à quête*. The very term clearly indicates that the young women employed there received payment mainly by passing a collection plate. It also served as a euphemism for *beuglant*—slang ("bellowing") meaning "concert hall" and also "low class"—which would hardly have appealed to an audience of officers. With admission free, spectators paid only for drinks.

1 It was at La Rotonde in Moulins that Gabrielle made her stage debut.
2 An 1885 announcement of the program of entertainment scheduled at La Rotonde.

PAVILLON DE LA ROTONDE
Place de la Gare
CONCERT
TOUS LES SOIRS A 8 HEURES
DIRECTION : Marguerite DAUMONT
DIMANCHE 18 OCTOBRE 1885
DÉBUTS
DE Mlle BÉNAC
Romancière des principaux Concerts de Paris
Continuation des REPRÉSENTATIONS de Mesdames
SUZANNE AUGIER
Comique de genre
THÉO
COMIQUE EXCENTRIQUE
MARGUERITE DAUMONT
Chanteuse légère
M. MOREL
Comique excentrique
M. Marius MAUGER
Pianiste accompagnateur
SAYNÈTES, DUOS, CHANSONS, CHANSONNETTES, ROMANCES, etc.
Dimanches et Jours de Fêtes MATINÉES MUSICALES de 2 h. 1/2 à 5 h.
Tous les jours Répétitions de 2 heures et demie à 4 heures et demie
ENTRÉE LIBRE
CONSOMMATIONS DE PREMIER CHOIX

they called her Coco

At Moulins in 1905 there still appeared on stage those concert-hall performers known as *poseuses* ("models")—actually supers who ranged themselves in a semicircle behind the stars and sat there like well-behaved guests at a *salon*. Their role was to give the establishment an air of gentility and to fill in between numbers. Whenever the stage emptied, one *poseuse* at a time would come forward and perform her own little piece, usually in a manner more dead than alive. This was how Chanel made her debut at La Rotonde, with a repertoire consisting of two songs: *"Ko Ko Ri Ko"* and *"Qui qu'a vu Coco."* The audience then began calling her by the word that appeared in the refrain of both songs. Soon she became *la petite Coco* to all her fans at the garrison.

1   Program for *Ko Ko Ri Ko*, a successful review produced by P.L. Flers in 1897 at La Scala, a chic *caf'conc'* in Paris.
2   H.G. Ibels, drawing, published in 1906. Narrow stage, upright piano, and, behind the star, a circle of ladies *en peaux* ("evening dress")—this was the *café-concert* formula.
3   Daumier, lithograph, Musée Bargouin, Clermont-Ferrand. Engaged by the month, dismissed after two weeks, bombarded with cherry pits—such was the unenviable lot of a music-hall beginner.
4   The music for *"Qui qu'a vu Coco,"* a ballad about the lost dog Coco composed by Elise Faure, comedy star, 1889.
5   Ibels, drawing for *Les Demi-Cabots* ("The Semi-Actors"), published in 1906. At La Rotonde in 1904 one of the *poseuses* passing among the tables with her collection plate, a practice long abandoned in the *café-concerts* of Paris.
6   Striking up the chorus of *Les Cuirassiers de Reichshoffen* was obligatory in concert halls catering

Premier sujet d'un café-concert, chantant de sept heures à minuit, avec ou sans roulades, selon le goût des consommateurs.

QUI QU'A VU COCO.
COMPLAINTE CANINE
Créée par Mme E. FAURE, aux Ambassadeurs.

Paroles de
AUMAINE et BLONDELET.

Musique de
ED. DERANSART.

1er
COUPLET.

J'ai per-du mon pauvr' Co-co Co-co
mon chien que j'a-do-re Tout près du Tro-ca-dé-
ro Il est loin s'il court en-co-re De l'a-
voue, mon plus grand r'gret Dans ma per-te si cru-
el-le, C'est qu'plus mon homm' me trom-pait... Plus Co-
REFRAIN
co m'é-tait fi-dè-le! Vous n'au-riez pas vu Co-co?
Co-co dans l'Tro-ca-dé-ro Co dans l'Tro-
Co dans l'Tro Co-co dans l'Tro-ca-dé-ro.
Qui qu'a qui qu'a vu Co-co? Eh! Co-co Eh! Co-co!
Qui qu'a qui qu'a vu Co-co? Eh! Co-co!

LES CUIRASSIERS DE REICHSHOFFEN
Chanté par Mme BORDAS, au Grand concert Parisien.
Paroles de MM. H. NAZET et VILLEMER;
Musique de Francis CHASSAIGNE.
La musique chez MM. GERARD et Cie, 12, b. des Capucines.

Ils reculaient, nos soldats invincibles,
A Reichshoffen, la mort fauchait leurs rangs;
Nos ennemis, dans les bois, invisibles,
Comme des loups poursuivaient ces géants.
Depuis le jour disputant la bataille,
France! ils portaient ton drapeau glorieux!
Ils sont tombés, vaincus par la mitraille,
Et non par ceux qui tremblaient devant eux!
    Voyez là-bas, comme un éclair d'acier,
    Ces escadrons passer dans la fumée,
    Ils vont mourir, et pour sauver l'armée
    Donner le sang du dernier cuirassier. (bis.)

On leur a dit : Il faut sauver la France
C'est de vous seuls que dépend l'avenir!
De Waterloo, gardez la souvenance ;
Ainsi qu'alors il faut vaincre ou mourir!
Le vent du soir, soulevant leurs crinières,
Et secouant leurs cuirasses d'airain,
Fit tressaillir au fond de leurs tanières,
Ces Allemands qui se serraient en vain.
    Voyez là-bas, etc.

Par quatre fois, torrent irrésistible,
Ce flot humain troua les rangs pressés
Des Allemands, que cet élan terrible
Sur les verts prés couchait comme les blés.
Ils sont passés ! mais après la bataille,
Quand on chercha ces régiments de fer,
Les corbeaux noirs faisaient déjà ripaille
De sang fumant et de lambeaux de chair !
    Ils sont là-bas, ces régiments d'acier
    Qu'on vit jadis à travers la fumée,
    Pour essayer de sauver notre armée,
    Donner le sang du dernier cuirassier. (bis.)
Toute reproduction est interdite.

CONCERT
Tous les soirs à huit heures
SOUS LA DIRECTION DE M. BODARD
DÉBUTS
DE
Mlle FRANCINE
COMIQUE DE GENRE
ET DE
Mlle NANA
COMIQUE

to a military audience. Wearing a *képi*, an *artiste* led the songs most favored by the uniformed patriots.
7 Daumier, lithograph, Musée Bargouin. "Every evening, the *artiste* must sing in evening dress." This regulation applied to the *poseuses* as well.
8 Poster-program for Le Bodard, Moulins' second *café-concert*, which in Chanel's time competed with La Rotonde.

the nobodies of Vichy

Among other things to know about the Chanel family, Gabrielle's grandfather, when an old man, sired a daughter who was the same age as his granddaughter. This made the beautiful Adrienne the aunt of Gabrielle, even though she was often taken as the latter's sister. From the age of seventeen, the two young women were inseparable, sharing the life of charity pupils, the life of shop girls, and even the stage at La Rotonde, where Adrienne, deemed to possess no vocal talent whatever, took charge of passing the plate. Thus, Adrienne followed when Gabrielle, who had great ambitions and dreamed of one day becoming the equal of Yvette Guilbert, left the Moulins *café-concert* for the "season" at Vichy, there to try her luck among the many music halls in what was France's most cosmopolitan watering place.

1   Gabrielle (left) and Adrienne (right) Chanel at Vichy in 1906, wearing dresses and hats made entirely by themselves. This constitutes the earliest known document in which the Chanel style can be sensed.
2   Built under Napoleon III, the casino with its iron-and-glass architecture—which anticipated the modern style—was the center of all the spa's fashionable events.
3   The lacy iron skeleton of the Galerie des Machines, dismantled and moved from Paris after the 1900 World's Fair, provided a covered walkway for the lovely promenaders of Vichy.
4   La Restauration, an open-air café at Vichy for those eager to be seen. Among the ladies assembled for the cure, one has only to note the big, heavy hats to appreciate what the Chanel style, beginning in 1906, would mean.

a slightly perverse charm

In Belle Époque Vichy it was believed that music,
light or classical, possessed curative powers at
least equal to those of the mineral waters. Thus,
the thermal season brought a veritable explosion
of concerts. In the morning, a performance in the
bandstand situated next to the spring known as
La Source de l'Hôpital; in the afternoon, another
one at the sidewalk cafés; and in the evening, four
variety theatres offering the best of France's *fan-
taisistes*.

1   The façade of the Élysée Palace, one of Vichy's
café-concerts at the beginning of the century.
2   At La Crèmerie, in the shade of Vichy's new
park, who are these ladies? Chanel, on the left,
with one of her sisters in 1907.
3   There is no doubt that Gabrielle Chanel tried
more than one line of work in Vichy. Concert-hall
engagements could not be picked up there as eas-
ily as in Moulins. But Gabrielle did receive some
hope that she might eventually become a *gommeuse*
("licker of envelopes," slang for a promising beginner, but in this instance on the music-hall
stage), if only she could develop her voice. The
gommeuse typically wore a spangled dress with a
bodice that lent fullness to the bust. After hugging
the hips, the skirt flared slightly to midcalf. A *gommeuse* had to be *décolletée* and show her legs. The
somewhat perverse seductiveness of this costume—the charm of a style neither long nor
short—would haunt and inspire Coco Chanel for
the rest of her life.

gommeuse without a future

1 *Adieu Paris!* Since she had abandoned all hope of a stage career in the capital and since success otherwise remained elusive, Gabrielle Chanel had no choice but to accept the provinces and to live there as best she could. Here, therefore, is Gabrielle at a crucial moment in her life. It is Sunday at the races in Vichy, with Chanel wearing a dress and hat made by herself. Does one see only Chanel? If so, it is because a complete naturalness sets her apart from the other women. Also because her hat would seem smart even today. Clearly, she is ready to bury those costly bird coffins with which her neighbors have dressed their heads. Moreover, Chanel alone wears her hair over the brow. In 1907 she inaugurated the fringe that would become the hair style of every emancipated woman of the 1920s. But note also the collar—the eternal little white collar, unrecognized but already a Chanel trademark. Nearby is Adrienne, a less daring figure, who conforms to the fashion of the day.

2 Not in the box of the landed gentry but among the bourgeois of the region. Adrienne, on the left, in jabot and high style; Gabrielle, on the right, simply clothed with a turned-down collar; and, between them, a new, opulent figure, her stature and her plume towering over all else. This is Maud, a friend of the Chanel girls who would play the complex role of counselor, duenna, and chaperone to Adrienne.

Adrienne
and her chaperone

When the season at Vichy came to an end and the *café-concerts* closed without even the smallest contract having been offered, the young Gabrielle no longer had any illusions: a stage career would not be hers. Thus, she gave up the idea of the theatre and returned to Moulins and to her old life—evenings at La Rotonde and flirtation with cavalry officers.

Still, a great change had come about. Adrienne, Gabrielle's young aunt and childhood friend, no longer resided in Moulins. She remained in the district, but living at Souvigny, in the home of an intimate friend, Maud Mazuel. Without taking Adrienne away from her original "cavalier" entourage, Maud had introduced her to some of the château nobility, older than the lieutenants of the 10th Chasseurs, but endowed with greater means and more freedom. Maud, although not beautiful, had spirit, self-assurance, and, when necessary, the air of a woman of rank, whose identification with the past was evident in her Louis XV jabots, her hats *à la mousquetaire,* and the cut of her suits, with their long slanting coattails reminiscent of the Directoire period.

Maud divided herself between two contradictory vocations: life of any party and chaperone. She was equally skilled in both roles.

A *demoiselle,* Maud had a great appetite for society and a keen desire to succeed in it. Born to a different milieu, she would have maintained a *salon,* but her obscure origins rendered this impossible. Thus, she made do by arranging encounters and perhaps in facilitating liaisons.

Adrienne used Maud as a means to ends that would otherwise have been unimaginable. In the person of her hostess, duly whaleboned, corseted, sheathed, and hatted, Adrienne found the indispensable duenna, the ideal chaperone without whom a young woman such as she—child of the people, devoid of means or family, yet ambitious, however foolishly, to enter society—would not have had the slightest chance of success. Maud would be the solid guarantee of Adrienne's respectability.

1   Adrienne (left) and Maud (right) in 1909 at a photographer's studio.

the mad love of Adrienne

1 To everyone in Vichy who saw her attending the races in a fine carriage, ravishingly turned out, and always in the company of a young man of old family, Adrienne appeared to be a woman of infinite daring.

2 J. Veber, *Chez la modiste*, lithograph, 1907. A cumbersome hat—so utterly an obligation at the time that it seemed less a fashion than a class distinction.

3 Coincidence? In Vichy, Adrienne adopted the ample ostrich plumes and large felt form worn by Cécile Sorel in 1911 when, for the Comédie-Française, she played the lead in a revival of *Le Demi-Monde*, the comedy of 1850 by Dumas *fils*. Judged "immoral and shocking" when first produced, the play was now accepted without difficulty, thanks to the art of la Sorel in the role of a *coquette*—beautiful, frivolous, delightful, and a bit fierce.

2

3

Mlle Cécile Sorel
Sociétaire de la Comédie-Française
dans le "Demi-Monde"

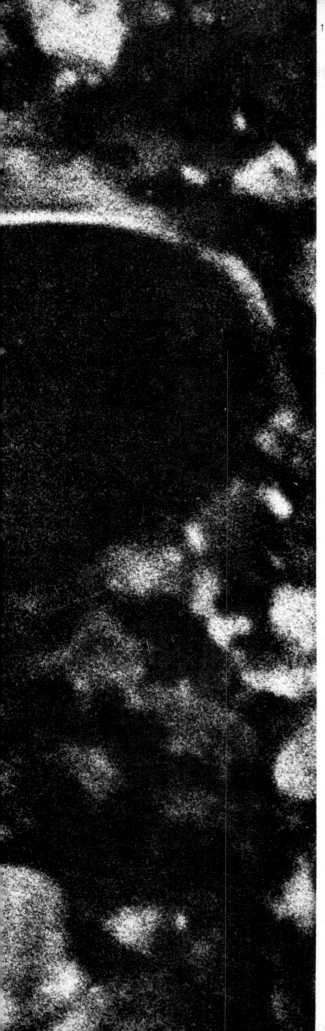

masters and mistresses

1   Chanel was twenty-five when she agreed to live with Étienne Balsan, the man who would lead her out of provincial backwaters and into château life. How could she have imagined that the new situation would offer so little change from all that she had wanted to escape in Moulins? On the delicate face under the immense black hat can be detected the traces of a bitter disappointment.

2   Suzanne Orlandi, a friend of Gabrielle's and the ravishingly beautiful mistress of Baron Foy.

3   In 1907 at Robinson, an outing on donkey-back for horsemen (breeders, trainers) and their *petites amies*. From left to right: Maurice Caillaux and Mademoiselle Forchemer, Suzanne Orlandi and Baron Foy, Chanel and Balsan. The pluckiness of Gabrielle's little bowtie offers a kind of male simplicity in contrast to the boned collars and Henri II ruffs that still encumber the other *amazones*.

Suzanne or the *demi-monde*

The lovely Suzanne Orlandi was typical of the young friends about whom Gabrielle, once she had become the famous Mademoiselle Chanel, would never speak. Perhaps it was because their fate had many points in common with hers. Suzanne Orlandi proved more than discreet concerning the misery of their youth, their struggles, their disappointments, the affronts they suffered—and discreet on the subject of their love affairs. Not a word would she utter. But this made her no less an irrefutable witness, which, in the mind of Gabrielle, constituted sufficient reason never to invoke the name of Suzanne Orlandi. Both belonged to that social category situated between *le monde*, the world qualifying as "society," and the other realm known as *le monde de la galanterie*. In other words, they occupied the *demi-monde*—the "half-world"—a term that came into general usage with the successful play of that title by Dumas *fils*. And the author had taken pains to give the definition that appeared in the dictionary as soon as the word had been created: "The *demi-monde*? A comedown for women who have left a high place, a summit for those who have left a low one." Gabrielle and Suzanne started from the bottom. And a woman of this half-world could expect nothing but a half-reality. It was imperative that she live unacknowledged, because, in the eyes of families, she was a greater threat than the celebrated courtesans who haunted Maxim's. These, at least, played a very straightforward game; they were paid and for the services rendered no one expected them to be sweet, simple, and good. Whereas a young, unknown woman? A man could become so infatuated that he might be persuaded to offer the respectability of marriage. Horrors! Marry a nobody without fortune, family, or even a *couturier*—a parvenue who dressed herself and made her own hats!

Coco, however, enjoyed one bit of good luck: Balsan did not have to suffer the opprobrium of relatives. Having been orphaned, he could live with Coco as he wished. Meanwhile, Suzanne as well as Adrienne would suffer endless humiliation. The families of the men they loved refused to receive them. Any trip they made in the company of their lovers had to be to a country where *le monde* never went, owing to its distance, danger, or discomfort. Thus, both Suzanne and Adrienne found themselves traveling in the only direction then possible under the circumstances—to Africa. There, however, one could be at peace, for neither the habitués of the Deauville boardwalks nor the great huntsmen of Chantilly would have ventured so far.

1   Born of a richly maintained opera singer and a father whose identity could never be disclosed, Suzanne loved to adopt theatrical attitudes and disguises. Here she is in a burnoose posing in the Aurès Mountains of Algeria.
2   Near Negrine during a voyage to Algeria, Suzanne Orlandi with Baron Foy.

Émilienne,
courtesan and poet

EMILIENNE D'ALENÇON

Sous le Masque

PARIS
BIBLIOTHÈQUE INTERNATIONALE D'ÉDITION
Edward SANSOT, Éditeur
7, RUE DE L'ÉPERON, 7
1918

Requiescat in Pace

à *Alec Carter*
mort au champ d'honneur (1914).
(Qu'il repose en paix !).

Où donc repose-t-il à présent, l'être cher ?
Dans le creux de quel arbre ou sous quelle colline ?
Quel oreiller soutient son beau visage clair ?
Sur quels draps argileux crispe-t-il ses mains fines ?

Who was Émilienne d'Alençon? For some, a brave girl; for others, a monster. In reality, she was the child of *concièrges* in the Rue des Martyrs who earned a special place among the great hetaeras reigning at the turn of the century. *La petite Coco*, a young unknown barely out of her native province, was presented to Émilienne in the home of Étienne Balsan.

Balsan, at the time of his encounter with Gabrielle Chanel, had the air of a young man of means making his mark in all the fashionable places. And he took a not inconsiderable pride in the mastery with which he had succeeded in casting off Émilienne after a whirlwind affair. Of all the courtesans of the era, this one was reputed to have the most voracious appetites.

Did she not, without batting an eye, ruin the young Duc d'Uzès? Moreover, there was no one in Paris who did not know for a fact that eight members of the Jockey Club had pooled their resources and formed a kind of corporation whose sole purpose was to secure the lady's favors on a regular basis. But all that had finished by 1907, and thereafter the famous *femme fatale* no longer had any interest in seizing the assets of ducal heirs or the family jewels of an old, bearded sovereign. Having made her fortune, Émilienne wanted only to amuse herself. Actually, while still a great favorite of the scandal sheets, she had become a bit *passée* in the *demi-monde*. At thirty-three, Émilienne found one of her latest passions in Alec Carter,

the jockey with three hundred victories to his credit and the idol of the whole turf crowd.

1 Portrait of Alec Carter at the time he was called "invincible."
2 Émilienne had literary ambitions as well. This collection of poems appeared in 1918.
3 Alec Carter, although English, enlisted in the French forces in 1914, only to be killed on October 11 of the same year.
4 The poem by Émilienne d'Alençon dedicated to the memory of Alec Carter.
5 The courtesan at the peak of her glory. One soon forgot that she was the daughter of *concièrges* and had been christened simply Émilienne André.

a certain idea of the body

By 1909 Gabrielle Chanel had developed into
this beauty with the heavy, dark hair, the small,
turned-up nose, the marvelous profile, a
young woman who was just now beginning to
make a name for herself. She sits straight, as
she would all her life, perched on every chair
as if on horseback, or as if by wearing an easier,
more fluid dress than those of her contemporaries, she had already become convinced that
being fit counted for more than a corset. This
was radical, her idea of the body. If Chanel did
not yet know quite what she wanted, her infal-
lible instinct told her precisely what she did *not*
want. All the fashions of the day, with their
complicated graces, struck her as ridiculous.
She was four years ahead of her time.

1 An *élégante* at the Longchamps races, 1913.
2 Cécile Sorel in *Vouloir* at the Comédie-
Française, 1913.
3 Gilda Darthy, a heady performer maintained on a grand scale by a Rothschild, 1912.
4 Madame Mona Delza, a star of the Vaudeville Theatre, 1912.
5 Chanel in 1909, with neither pearls nor
lace. Under her dress she wears a *modestie*
trimmed with ribbon, as simple and attractive
as a convent pinafore.

1

a youthful air

1 Gabrielle Chanel was twenty-six when, standing on a bench at a racecourse in the Midi, with binoculars hung bandolier-style, she watched the training of one of the Balsan horses. Everything about her is simple, fashionless, and *sportive*. She had made herself a little hat suited to the circumstances and secured with a huge pin against the blustery winds of the mistral. If she has a jaunty look, it is thanks to the coat borrowed from Baron Foy and the tie from Balsan, both of whom were astounded by her mania for stealing their clothes! But little could Coco imagine that her improvised ensemble constituted the first draft of a style that, twenty years later when she had become a renowned *couturière*, would have all women wearing white collars, neckties, and boaters.
2 The little boater, born in 1910 on a windy day, would always be her favorite type of hat, and she made it the height of fashion for half a century.
3 Women and fashions that Coco avoided.
4 Émilienne d'Alençon in straw boater and wing collar.

2

defying fashion

Going from track to track—this was how one lived with Étienne Balsan. But Coco had to keep to the grass, since she could not risk encountering some lady or other who might be offended by the sight of the woman Balsan was living with. In her obsessive fear of being taken for a *cocotte*, Gabrielle observed the proprieties to excess. At all cost, she had to set herself apart from everyone else in her position. Thus, she could have been taken for the most straightforward of young women, coiffed in one of the straw boaters she made for herself and that enchanted her friends. One of Coco's hats caught the fancy of Émilienne d'Alençon, after which the great courtesan never wore anything but boaters, although overloading them with a thousand personal embellishments. From now on there was no denying the influence of Gabrielle Chanel, which grew until it reached beyond her circle of friends.

5 Cécile Sorel coiffed in a plumed boater.
6 Émilienne d'Alençon, who added a big ribbon to her straw hat.

the fun-loving Balsan crowd

Among other advantages, Balsan's hospitality was open to everything but snobbery. Étienne had banished the whole lot of virtuous wives and formidable dowagers, and allowed everyone to live sheltered from what Proust called "the pitiless glare of lorgnettes." Whom did he gather about him? Mainly stars of sport and theatre, all free spirits who did not count "virtue" among the foremost of their qualities, but who otherwise were more attractive than the milieu in which Gabrielle had begun her independent social life in Moulins and Vichy.

Among the habitués of Balsan's household could be found a second and brilliant Gabrielle in the person of a young actress then just making her mark: Gabrielle Dorziat. Another, but talentless, actress was Jeanne Lery, whom the Grand Duke Boris had abandoned after a long liaison. As for the men, they formed a band of horse lovers who fully appreciated a household in which it was possible to enjoy the rare pleasure of living freely with their mistresses. All of Balsan's friends—male and female—participated in their host's favorite pastime, which consisted of producing home-made farces and arranging grand entrances in disguise, with the events recorded by camera.

1 Here one morning, a bathrobed Gabrielle Chanel reads her paper after having appeared at breakfast disguised as a *chaisière* (chair attendant in the park).
2 One evening the Balsan group improvised *Une Noce campagnarde* ("A Country Wedding"), a production costumed by Gabrielle. From left to right: Gabrielle as best man, Balsan, Lery as the bride and Henraux as the groom, and Arthur Capel as mother-in-law. Seated: Comte de Laborde playing the newlyweds' baby and Gabrielle Dorziat the maid of honor. On Capel's head note the ribbon "cabbage" that Gabrielle had worn as the *chaisière*. At Balsan's a good time could be had at little expense to anyone.

laughter replaces luxury

The change is evident, for even in their amusements the Balsan crowd challenged the Belle Époque. With them a whole era of Parisian life came to an end, an era that had turned frivolity into a costly apotheosis. Even though Balsan had certainly slept with Émilienne d'Alençon, she was already, in the eyes of his friends, a person from another age.

1 At an Opéra ball, Émilienne dressed as Columbine, coiffed in a cocked hat of fresh flowers and adorned with her famous three-strand necklace of pearls.
2 The two Gabrielles, Dorziat and Chanel, as maid and man of honor at a village wedding, dressed in what Chanel had been able to purchase at the most popular of the period's great stores: La Samaritaine. Had a woman of fashion dared set foot there, the newspapers would have sent photographers. But what is it that seems so modern about these figures? Taken from the pages of

4 an album, this yellowed photograph, which dates from 1912, raises the curtain upon our time.

3 Here Chanel impersonates a timid adolescent boy, escorting Dorziat's village girl whose socks are too short and whose skirt is too long. For Gabrielle, the jacket worn over a white vest, the shirt with its Peter Pan collar and its cuffs extended beyond the coat sleeves, the softly knotted bowtie, the white "Breton" hat with its turned-up brim, the snowy gloves slipped into the breast pocket, no doubt for the want of a handkerchief—all this, bought in the boys' department of a large store, constitutes a sketch for what would become the Chanel style. While playing a game, Gabrielle had discovered the fundamental principle of her art: elements of male attire adapted for feminine use.

4 At the height of the Belle Époque it was considered extremely daring for a woman to appear on the stage in tight *culottes*. When Émilienne d'Alençon took the risk, she was the first, doing so in 1889 at the Cirque d'Été. Here she is in 1910, a rather buxom Harlequin with heavy thighs and a quilted doublet ornamented with bells.

château life

5 To receive an invitation to Royallieu, a woman had to be fun-loving, capable of wearing boots the whole time, and willing to gallop all day long from one end of the forest to the other. Gabrielle Chanel, having become the mistress of Étienne Balsan, found herself living intimately with a man who was the very incarnation of the sportsman type, oblivious to the world except that part of it where horses raced, seeing only a few close friends, ladies of the *demi-monde,* and jockeys.

The Château de Royallieu was at the center of a region where horses counted for more than anything else. Balsan took up residence there, for an article of faith held that a thoroughbred, in order to realize its promise, had to be trained in the Compiègne region and nowhere else. Here could be found whole dynasties of trainers who had come from England and established themselves in France. Chantilly and Maisons-Lafitte were now veritable English villages. Horses and horses alone—Balsan gave them the greatest part of his time and resources, and undoubtedly his stables ranked among the best in France. As for Gabrielle at Royallieu, her expectations were not excessive, but she insisted on having them all and immediately: to sleep as long as she wished, to become the best horsewoman at Royallieu, and to think of nothing—in other words, to beat the Balsan crowd at their own game. She succeeded marvelously.

6

1 At Royallieu, reading the newspapers every morning on the terrace was an immutable rite. All the dailies of the period devoted an entire page to news of the turf and several columns to a minute description of the latest outfits worn by the *cocottes,* the true queens of *le Tout-Paris.* From left to right: Chanel in a suit, *claudine* or "school girl" collar, and a white *lavallière;* Lucien Henraux in leggings reading *Le Journal;* and Gabrielle Dorziat wearing a riding habit while immersed in *L'Excelsior.*
2 Royallieu was once an abbey whose park had been planted with splendid trees.
3 Tall windows assured beautifully illuminated interiors.
4 The charm of a handsome provincial residence.
5 Wild deer roamed freely in the meadows.
6 The thick mass of Gabrielle's hair was gathered at the nape of her neck in a sumptuous chignon.

in the horse country

By reason of a natural shyness as much as for pleasure, Chanel spent the first months of her stay at Royallieu without leaving the estate. Actually, everything about the château overwhelmed her: the beauty of the park, the scale of the house and its stables, the luxury that surpassed all she had ever known.

1   Gabrielle Chanel in 1912. By stripping her wardrobe of every embellishment, she hoped to escape the reputation she most dreaded: that of the kept woman. Still, Chanel became Balsan's *irregulière* ("irregular" because not married to the man she lived with) in the eyes of all who viewed her isolation as proof that she had something to hide.
2   The abbey, although rebuilt in the 17th century by Benedictine nuns, had been founded by monks in 1303.
3   The stables built by Étienne Balsan.
4   Gabrielle Chanel with Baron Foy.
5   The gatehouse at Royallieu.
6   In the stairway, the portrait of Gabrielle de Laubespine, the first Abbess of Royallieu.
7   Dorziat in riding habit. She wears a headband of white piqué like those common among women in tennis. Created by Gabrielle, such a headpiece for galloping through the forest was deemed pure bad taste by society horsewomen who preferred *tricornes* or top hats.

2

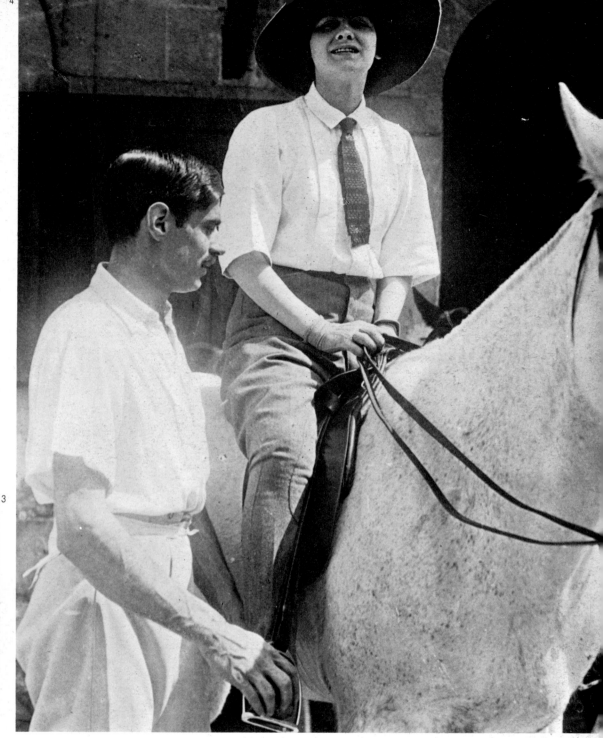

the stables dethrone the paddock

"Chanel had only to appear in order to make the whole prewar mode fade away, causing Worth and Paquin to wither and die. She was a shepherdess. To her, the training course, boot leather, hay, horse dung, the forest interior, saddle soap all smelled sweet." This is how Paul Morand, a friend and confidant, expressed Chanel's attitude. Then he added that Gabrielle belonged to "that advanced guard of country girls in underskirts and flat shoes characterized by Marivaux, girls who go out, confront the dangers of the city, and triumph, doing so with the kind of solid appetite for vengeance that revolutions are made of." With Chanel began an elegance in reverse, which brought an end to parade clothes. She would not join the women who caracoled along the Avenue du Bois or those who strutted in the enclosures that were forbidden to her. The day was coming when simplicity would prevail in a world where women, as Chanel phrased it herself, had once been nothing but an excuse for embellishment, for laces, etc. According to Chanel, the stables would dethrone the paddock.

1 At the Deauville Grand Prix in 1907, women leaving the paddock.
2 Morning along the Avenue du Bois in 1912. The proud parade of corseted horsewomen, riders in top hats, beautiful mounts, the finest *equipages*, the most recent automobiles. It all made a perfect elegance reigning over a splendid *ennui*.
3 At the stables of Royallieu, equestrians in shirtsleeves. Gabrielle, still afraid to expose her face to the sun, wears what is nothing but a large felt hat-form, pulled down over the ears. With her are the elegant Léon de Laborde, at center, and Étienne Balsan.
4 Boy Capel, Balsan's best friend, and Chanel on horseback. An outrage in the eyes of the fashionable world, Chanel wears jodhpurs, the model for which she obtained from a groom and had copied by a local tailor.

changing her way of life

All of Balsan's friends noticed it. During the spring of 1912 an intimate friend of Étienne, but a new habitué at Royallieu, appeared at the château with increasing frequency, all the while showing more and more interest in the charms of Gabrielle Chanel. The group had expanded to include an Englishman with thick, black hair, a charmer whom every woman adored and who pursued the life of a self-made man. His name was Arthur Capel, but friends called him "Boy." In Boy, Gabrielle Chanel found what she had vainly sought in Balsan—help and encouragement. Between Gabrielle and Étienne had arisen the first dissension concerning the eagerness she now felt to change her way of life. What did she want? To work. Her idleness weighed on Coco. She was bored. She wanted to go to Paris and make a career for herself as a *modiste*—a milliner. It was not that Étienne opposed the idea, but that he pretended to see the project as nothing more than a lark, whereas Gabrielle spoke in terms of a real *métier*. She did not wish merely to amuse herself concocting hats for friends, but rather to sell the creations and make a name for herself. Only Boy saw merit in the idea.

1 Scene of feigned jealousy in morning *déshabille*. Arthur Capel, in satin kimono, menacing Léon de Laborde in short pajamas. In his arms, Gabrielle wrapped in a bathrobe, her beautiful, long hair falling about her shoulders.
2 Photos taken early in the summer of 1912. Breakfast at Royallieu, the happy band of equestrians: Boy (from the back), Léon de Laborde (left), Gabrielle Dorziat, Balsan, Lucien Henraux, Gabrielle Chanel, and Jeanne Lery.

life with Boy

In high society and in Paris most of all, the French were anglophobes in politics while sheer snobbery made them anglophiles in their way of life. This helps explain the surprising popularity of Arthur Capel in Paris. What did anyone know about him? He had spent the greater part of his youth in English boarding schools: Beaumont, a Jesuit institution for the sons of Catholic gentlemen, and then Downside, run by the Benedictines and somewhat less uppercrust in social standing. But a great mystery surrounded his birth. Never did Boy mention his mother. Allegedly he was the natural son of a Frenchman who died shortly before Boy had finished his studies. This gave him something in common with Chanel: orphanhood. As for the identity of his father, the name most often proposed was Pereire. Boy Capel may have been the bastard of the great banker and, moreover, a bit Jewish. But it was known for certain that in London, Boy had been received in the most restricted circles. Thus, because the English appreciated his rare abilities in polo and found it amusing and original that he took pleasure in working and earning money, Parisians resolved to do as much, to the point where no one bothered about the secrets of his birth. Personal attractiveness and his skill at cultivating the interests he owned in the coal fields of Newcastle simply added to the prestige enjoyed by Boy Capel.

1 Arthur Capel in his ground-floor apartment on the Boulevard Malesherbes in Paris. With him Gabrielle Chanel discovered that one could be both a champion polo player and a lover of literature.
2 Boy in Morocco. Marshal Lyautey, who made Morocco a French protectorate, had not been in Fez a full year when Capel was already investing, and also talking about making Casablanca a great port for the importation of English coal.

To set Chanel up in Paris presented a number of problems, and Étienne Balsan hesitated. Buy her a business? He laughed at the opinion of others—Boy's for instance—as long as the little nobody from Vichy lived discreetly. Maintaining and living with a mistress could actually gain him a certain prestige. But allow her to work? What a scandal! Then, too, like so many former cavalry officers, he liked spending money only so long as it was for horses. In the end, Étienne thought to solve the problem by offering Chanel, in lieu of a professional space, the *garçonnière*, or "bachelor's chambers," that he owned on the ground floor at 160 Boulevard Malesherbes. Foolish man! Boy lived nearby, and right away he began making neighborly calls. Chanel, charming and still dressed like a boarding-school girl, simply drank in all he had to say. Moreover, success did not long wait to embrace Coco's millinery efforts. Women were mad about Chanel hats. The beauteous friends of Balsan and Boy seemed to fall over one another to buy the little orphan's boaters. Boy offered prodigies of advice, all the while that Balsan grew more annoyed. His best friend taking *work* seriously, and the work of Gabrielle! Finally, the reason for Capel's *parti pris* became shockingly clear: Boy was in love with Coco. What was more, he admitted it. Balsan played the good prince and continued to let Gabrielle have the *garçonnière*, although he knew that she was now living with Boy. Coco even returned to Royallieu with him, but only as a guest. She seemed to be a different woman.

3   Under a bowler hat, Chanel's ponytail was a shattering audacity. Even when dressed for riding, an elegant woman could not give up her "ratted," raised, and heavily supplemented coiffure.
4   The well-cut riding habit worn by Chanel indicated, all by itself, that a change had occurred in her life.

pages 66–67   Coco Chanel, Étienne Balsan, and Boy Capel.

an irresistible man

Gabrielle Chanel stated upon a number of occasions that she had loved but once in her life and only once had known a man who seemed created for her: Arthur Capel. And it is almost certain that for once she spoke the truth.

Chanel loved everything about Capel. "More than handsome," she said, "he was magnificent." Coco admired everything about him, his eyes that looked at her with authority, his black hair, so deep a black that it seemed to make his face look encircled in jet. She even liked his foreign accent, also his feigned nonchalance. "He had a very strong, very individual personality, an ardent and concentrated nature." Never before could she have imagined life with a man who was at once athletic, enterprising, literate, and, despite his youth, already an important businessman. Gabrielle, of course, had known only young men more gifted in diminishing their fortunes than in adding to them.

Until then Chanel had lived happily enough, but always with the secret hope of breaking free of the mediocre role to which she had been limited first by the self-centered and frivolous officers at Moulins and then, at Royallieu, by Étienne Balsan, who, while certainly a decent fellow with a sincere affection for her, was idle and too preoccupied with his horses and his equestrian success to take seriously the aspirations of his beautiful companion.

Finished were the band of crazy friends and the gallops through the forest. Soon to be finished also was Coco Chanel's work as a *modiste* in inadequate quarters whose address could not inspire confidence. At the beginning, of course, *la mode en garçonnière* seemed irresistibly amusing, for Gabrielle as much as for the carefree habitués of Royallieu. In February 1910 Coco had been encamped there a year, lodged at the expense of Étienne on the Boulevard Malesherbes, where she made do in the cramped space of a ground-floor apartment. But despite the problems of such an arrangement, Chanel saw her clientele increase day by day: "The customers simply arrived, at first out of curiosity. One day I received a visit from a lady who frankly admitted: 'I've come . . . to see you.' I was a strange bird, a little lady with a boater on her head and her head on her shoulders."

passed through the hard school of Parisian ateliers. Each had submitted at a young age to training under a severe and demanding *première*. As a result, they knew all the subtleties of the trade. This was certainly not the case with Gabrielle Chanel, who had received no professional preparation whatever. A certain looseness prevailed in that first boutique, where the comings and goings proved enormously intriguing to a tradition-minded public. Sometimes it was the handsome Boy, sometimes Léon de Laborde, and then again it could be Balsan who dropped in to say *bonjour*. Unable to cope with the idea of a *modiste* pursued by so many men, the great ladies did not return. Chanel insisted that it took a long while for her to become aware of the curiosity she aroused: "I was extremely naïve. I hadn't the remotest notion that it was I they were looking at. I saw myself as nothing but a provincial girl like so many others. The time of the extravagant dresses I had dreamed about—the sort of dresses worn by heroines—no longer existed. I had never even had a convent uniform with a *pèlerine*, embellished with Holy Ghost or 'children of Mary' ribbons so beloved in childhood. I forgot about lace, for I knew nothing rich would become me. I had only my kid-skin coat and my poor little suits. Capel said to me: 'Since it means so much to you, I will have an English tailor remake *en elegant* what you wear all the time.' This was the origin of all that has happened in the Rue Cambon."

a generous lover

A question remained unanswered: To break or not? How could she forget what she owed to Étienne? The issue remained suspended for a while. Then reality had to be acknowledged: The honeymoon *à trois* was over. In order to act and build, Gabrielle needed a solid companion. And Arthur Capel was that companion: "For me he was brother, father, my whole family."

The transfer of power occurred without tears or scenes. It was a change of partners in the best tradition of French wit and style. With complete, natural ease, Capel simply took Balsan's place, at the same time that he advanced the funds necessary to purchase a business for Gabrielle.

In the last months of 1910 Gabrielle Chanel found herself lodged with Arthur Capel, in an elegant apartment on the Avenue Gabriel, and creating hats upstairs at number 21 in a street whose name would be associated with hers for half a century: the Rue Cambon. A plaque on the door read: *Chanel Modes*. At last Coco was an independent *milliner* at a professional address of her own choosing.

At first, Gabrielle had infinite difficulty adapting to the exigencies of business. She possessed little comprehension of how to deal with the pretty women who appeared for the first time and whom she knew to be clients of Reboux, Georgette, or Suzanne Talbot. These competitors, all famous, "arrived" women, had

a hero worthy of a novel

Of all Chanel's friends, Paul Morand was the one who had known Arthur Capel the best and unquestionably the one with whom she most enjoyed talking about this exceptional man. Morand himself had felt the fascination of Boy. And the two shared certain irresistible penchants, for fast living, for luxury, for success, for record-breaking sports, for horses, for worldly glitter, for quick conquest, and for adventurous women. Moreover, they had in common a great appetite for people and for life touched by a certain cynicism, even a dandyism, which was nothing more than a façade masking their fear of seeming too serious.

It should be no surprise that Boy became the subject of a novel. "This Lewis who somewhat recalls Boy Capel" was the dedication that Morand wrote in the copy of *Lewis et Irène* that Chanel kept in her library. A close reading reveals the character Lewis to have been drawn almost completely from Boy—"beautiful, quick brown eyes, a strong chin, and massively thick, black, unruly hair . . ."—and a bit of Coco in Irène: "You are a businesswoman because you know how to survive." In addition, throughout the book, and barely altered, there are numerous aspects of Coco's life with Boy in Paris, from the time of their first encounter: "They saw no one. People annoyed Irène. . . ." *Lewis et Irène* can, in large measure, be taken as a portrait of the Chanel-Capel liaison.

2

Chanel's first boutique

In 1912 the Théâtre du Vaudeville presented a play by F. Nozière entitled *Bel Ami* and based upon the novel by Guy de Maupassant. "A strongly applauded play," wrote the critic for *L'Illustration*, adding that "Gabrielle Dorziat acted with true and spontaneous naturalness." A more reserved judgment was that of the *Matin* reviewer, who wrote that "despite a certain talent, Mlle Dorziat had something a bit dry and strained in her playing. . . ." He signed himself "Launay," but his name was Léon Blum.

Unanimity, however, governed the opinion about Dorziat's costuming, which all critics found exquisite. She was in fact dressed by Jacques Doucet. If the beautiful Dorziat was to wear clothes from the greatest *couturiers* in the Rue de la Paix, why not let Chanel be the milliner? To persuade the actress, Coco sent one of their old friends from Royallieu, and little Jeanne Lery did not fail. Here was a unique opportunity, and Chanel had to grasp it. Dorziat allowed herself to be convinced, and she opened wearing hats signed "Chanel."

1 Chanel's large straw, without plumes or any other garnish, completed to perfection the splendid dress worn by the famous Gabrielle Dorziat in *Bel Ami*.
2 Gabrielle Dorziat in *Bel Ami*, wearing a hat by Chanel, who was making her debut as a designer for the theatre at the same time that she was also launching her first—modest—boutique in Paris.

first clients

In 1912 the pretty ladies who had adorned the Roy-allieu Sundays—the horsewomen, the high-spirited friends of Balsan—made an important place for themselves in the theatre. It was they—all of them admired, applauded, and more and more photographed for the fashion magazines—who would reveal to Paris the name of a young, unknown milliner: Gabrielle Chanel.

1   In the *Journal des modes* Dorziat wears a hat by Chanel, May 1912.
2   Dorziat wrapped in a coat by Révillon. Her *tricorne* is a creation by Chanel, 1912.
3   One said henceforth: "Mlle Dorziat of the Vaudeville." Here hatted by Chanel.
4   Advertising began to make use of the current stars. Here Jane Diris, star of the Vaudeville and future star of silent films, posing under the name of her husband, whom a handsome and luxurious album, *Les Robes de Paul Poiret dessinées par Paul Iribe*, had just launched.
5   Little Suzanne Orlandi, who caught the attention of Parisian gossip columnists because of her liaison with Baron Foy. Here she wears a hat from Chanel Modes and a dress created from instructions drawn up by her friend Gabrielle. It is made of black velvet with a little collar of airy petals in white lawn. Here already was the Chanel style, in what may be her first professional dress design, 1913.
6   The prestigious black coupé, its white-wall spare tire stowed like a life-buoy against the side of a beautiful ship, the proud air of the chauffeur—all that to advertise Triplex glass and the beauteous Gabrielle Dorziat.

taking on the three giants

It was not yet known that Chanel could make dresses. Only her talent for hats had been recognized. However, the word began to circulate, and one by one a few young socialites went to Coco for help with their wardrobes. The competitiveness this aroused in the little milliner stunned everyone. She truly felt ready to take on the giants of the trade.

7 Worth, as seen by Cappiello. *Couturier* to the entire *Almanach de Gotha,* Worth had executed an order from Countess Greffulhe for a nurse's smock made of Cluny lace and designed to be worn by the Countess at her daughter's lying-in.

8 At Deauville an *élégante* with Sem, the period's most dreaded caricaturist. A lady was supposed to be ample, well corseted, and lost under frills and furbelows.

9 Here caught by Cappiello, Jacques Doucet had begun as director of a modest lingerie shop, then became an immensely rich and successful *couturier* of international renown.

10 In 1912, a client of Madame Georgette, bristling with egret plumes and photographed by the Seeberger brothers.

11 Poiret as caricatured by Oberlé. Having commenced under Doucet and then Worth, Poiret was at the apogee of his career in 1912. His Oriental style with its "hobble skirt" (*jupe rattrapée*) became the rage.

12 In 1909 the Seeberger brothers opened the first photographic agency specializing in fashion pictures shot outdoors where high fashions were actually worn. They had an immediate success. This photograph was taken at the races in 1912.

hatmaker to the divas

In Paris no publication before 1914 exercised greater influence than *Les Modes*. The magazine had been launched in 1909 from the sumptuous Hôtel des Modes as part of a great exhibition to which *le Tout-Paris* had been invited. Here were assembled the creations of the *couturiers* and milliners, together with costly furniture and portraits by La Gandara and Paul Helleu of the period's most beautiful women. Now, in 1912, *Les Modes* announced with great fanfare the arrival of a new hat designer: Gabrielle Chanel. Full-page reproductions illustrated the Chanel hats chosen by such young and beautiful performers as Gabrielle Dorziat and the ravishing Geneviève Vix, an opera singer then drawing full houses at the Opéra-Comique for her appearances in *Manon*, *Werther*, and *Tosca*. Vix—like Dorziat, a friend of Coco's—had many points in common with the new millinery star. By the time the photograph on the fac-

ing page was published, Geneviève Vix had succeeded Gabrielle in the small apartment the latter long occupied at 160 Boulevard Malesherbes: the *garconnière* of the Balsans. All the while that Gabrielle was "protected" by Étienne Balsan, Geneviève had received the same attention from Jacques Balsan, Étienne's brother. Then, in 1920, when Chanel was living with Grand Duke Dmitri, a romance developed between Vix and Prince Kyril Narishkin, which placed both young women in the circle of *émigrés* from Tsarist Russia. But whereas Gabrielle Chanel would never marry, Prince Narishkin made Vix his wife, and Dorziat became Countess Zoghreb.

1 The great comedienne Gabrielle Dorziat in a Chanel hat.
2 The much admired and very gifted opera singer Geneviève Vix wearing another *chapeau* by Chanel.

town fashion as conceived by the great designers

Until 1905, a new dress model could be photographed only in the salon of its creator and by an "artistic photographer." Reutlinger, Félix, and Manuel immortalized the creations of the Callot sisters, Paquin, and Worth. Then, suddenly, the growing number of magazines, with all the attendant publicity such media fostered—a process that no one understood better than Poiret—changed everything, making possible the appearance, around 1910, of the first photographic agency specializing in outdoor camera work. By offering this service, the three Seeberger brothers gave birth to fashion reportage.

1 Photo by Seeberger. Fashion evolved more slowly than mores. Here, in 1912, an attempt at culotte-skirts did make walking easier. But what is that under the garment? A stiff corset, a whaleboned bodice, and possibly even a padded bosom.
And what about the hat? "It was grotesque. How could a brain function normally under all that?" asked Chanel much later, her implaca-

town fashion as conceived by Chanel

ble irony serving to give an opinion of those monumental, overloaded, headache-producing lids.

2   At Nice and very properly dressed in muff, veil, black-velvet hat, and a fitted, calf-length jacket, Coco Chanel was photographed on the Promenade des Anglais attended by her cohort of admirers: Monsieur de Yturbe, Léon de Laborde, and Étienne Balsan. The simple hat of a triumphant black—which made anachronisms of the overloads of gauze and plumes that still covered her contemporaries' heads—turned custom upside down and thus epitomized what distinguished Chanel and made her *different*. By now already an established milliner, she could answer the question "Who dresses you?" with a ready and unblushing "I do."

3   Adrienne at the races in Vichy. On her Coco tried out the hats that she would later put on the heads of her clients. Half a century later, Chanel said to Paul Morand: "The women I saw at the races were wearing enormous deepdish pies; but what horrified me most of all was that the hats did not fit down over the head."

an encounter
with Caryathis

A father who peddled in the street and chased skirts, a strong peasant heritage, a dressmaker mother from Auvergne, a convent childhood—what a lot Caryathis and Chanel had in common. With a sack on his back, the father of Carya sold small wares from village to village. Then having become a journeyman baker, he acquired a certain fame presiding over the ovens at Larue before disappearing forever as chef on board the Transiberian Railway. Like the mother of Coco, Carya's mother had therefore been an abandoned wife. And the hapless Caryathis, apprenticed at age fourteen to Paquin, lived through a joyless childhood. Was it their common past that drew Coco to Caryathis, or the desire to know a liberated woman?

1 The youthful Caryathis, who ran away from home and spent her meager earnings on riotous living. As a cancan dancer at the Bal Bullier, she joined the *vie de bohème* among the painters of Paris' Butte Montmartre.

2 Caryathis in Francis Poulenc's *Le Jongleur*. "Be imperious, take bounding leaps, tear yourself apart," Cocteau told her. The avant-garde Russian painter Larionov designed the costume.

3 A character dancer, Caryathis identified herself with the "eurhythmic school" of Jacques-Dalcroze. Here, dressed as a Greek courtesan, she dances *Thaïs*.

4 For her interpretation of Granados, Caryathis wore a costume designed by Natalia Gontcharova, Larionov's wife and a leading Russian painter in her own right. The dancer described the dress as "a great

circle of lace that allowed the movements of my body to be seen from the hips down."

5 At the time of the encounter between Chanel and Caryathis, Colette was experiencing the tough school of music hall. Divorced from Monsieur Willy, her hair cut short, and flouting every propriety in the mime-dramas produced by Georges Wague, she suffered the severest criticism from Parisian society.

6 But one woman had preceded Colette in her revolutionary path. This was Caryathis, another *déclassée*, who several years before had shocked her contemporaries when, in a fit of rage, she left most of her hair hanging on a nail to avenge herself upon a man whose ardor she had failed to arouse. As a consequence, she became one of the first women to appear in public with bobbed hair.

Now, Caryathis took Chanel as a pupil, for in 1912 the *modiste* had succumbed to one last theatrical temptation, this time to dance. Coco evidently felt unfulfilled in her original ambitions for the stage. But she would have no more success among the pupils of Caryathis than she did in the basement of cafés in Vichy eight years earlier.

Caryathis, at age eighty, remembered having received Coco in her studio on the Rue Lamarck, which, in addition to her to classes, had witnessed the teacher's tumultuous amours with the celebrated dancer Charles Dullin. Without the testimony of Caryathis, what would we know of the choreographic dreams of Coco Chanel, who felt the allure of a medium—eurhythmic dance, the invention of Dalcroze—that would enthrall Paris and even influence Diaghilev.

Montmartre, the capital of art

In Montmartre, the capital of art in the pre-World War I era, stood a dilapidated, moldy old tenement—mockingly called the Bateau-Lavoir after the laundry barges anchored in the Seine—that would become a veritable tinder box for the artistic explosion known as Cubism. Here lived Picasso, Gris, Modigliani, and Jacob, a few "men all by themselves, with no support other than their own keenness and daring, whose struggle other, hostile men stood back and watched. . . ." These words came from Pierre Reverdy, a poet and fellow denizen of the Bateau-Lavoir. Passionately ex-

cited over the artists' innovations and himself a precursor of the new poetry, Reverdy later wrote: "I pity those who, having lived through that marvelous period, failed to participate in it, sharing its often disheartening and painful trials, its incomparably powerful emotions, its spiritual felicity. I doubt that there has ever been so much blue sky and sun in the entire history of art, or so much responsibility heroically assumed. . . ."

1 *Nord-Sud*, the review that Reverdy created and directed, influenced the poetic sensibility of his time as decisively as did the experiments of Reverdy's friends the Cubists. So influential was the review that Joan Miró gave the title *Nord-Sud* to a still life that he painted in Barcelona in 1917, before he had been to Paris or met Pierre Reverdy.
2 A portrait bearing this dedication: "For Pierre Reverdy, his friend Picasso, 15.11.21."
3 Reverdy at the Bateau-Lavoir in 1912. Ardent and sensitive, Reverdy had, between 1920 and 1924, an affair with Chanel that was marked by violent quarrels and reconciliations. But even after their rupture, Reverdy, who had a warm admiration for Coco, never ceased to feel a lively friendship for her.

1913:
Chanel invents sports fashion

Because in 1913 women had neither fashions nor even clothing for sports, and because her contemporaries, as she phrased it, "attended sporting events the way women in hennins attended medieval tournaments," Chanel would invent a whole new style, for relaxation and outdoor living.

1 The pleasures of the Normandy coast around 1913—available only to the well-to-do. For the working classes, such recreations belonged to the realm of fantasy.

2 The pleasure-seekers did not so much bathe as flounder about, doing so despite the fact that clothing inhibited even this much activity. One went to Étretat as if to a city, dressed from head to toe. Chanel was right: "1914 was still 1900, and 1900 was still the Second Empire."

3 A young milliner on vacation at Étretat. "Chanel built her wardrobe in response to her needs, just the way Robinson Crusoe built his hut. . . ," wrote Paul Morand in *L'Allure de Chanel*. Indeed, she held onto some old-fashioned ideas so as to be better able to adopt forms until then considered too common for fashion, such as workclothes and fatigues. Here, her inspiration came from Norman fishermen.

4 The garment Chanel wears was made of tricot, a material never before used in fashion because it seemed totally unsuitable for tailoring, too poor and soft, good only for underwear.

Chanel's creative urge was subversive, for it rejected ceremony and all its oppressiveness.

the conquest of Deauville

Some ten months before war broke out, Gabrielle Chanel decided to open her first boutique and to do it in Deauville. The shop offered hats, to which very shortly their designer would add jumpers, jackets, and the *marinière*, or "sailor blouse," that became *the* war-time garment of all well-dressed ladies, who finally gave up their high, choker collars.

1 The first photograph of a *couturière* named Chanel, standing in front of her first boutique and wearing clothes signed by herself. Linen skirt, sailor blouse, open collar, and simple hat—all her first official creations. On the left, Adrienne—also dressed by Chanel and a living advertisement for the designer.
2 Deauville on the eve of world conflict. The beach was left to maids and children, who had permission to make mud pies. The sea existed only to be looked at. One man even wears a top hat.
3 Adrienne facing the water, accompanied by her faithful admirer, her little dogs, and Maud Mazuel, still in service as *dame de compagnie*.

the Chanel ladies

Here was fashion in the year 1913 at Deauville, when Chanel, financed by Boy Capel, opened a boutique in the center of town. The exact location was Rue Gontaut-Biron, a chic street *par excellence*. Chanel employed a pair of youngsters who were only sixteen years old and hardly knew how to sew. No matter! The new *couturière* set to work.

1 Adrienne on the boardwalk. Every day she went to the Chanel boutique, borrowed dresses and hats, different ones each time, and by showing herself about town, not only became the object of great attention but also helped double Coco's business. Thanks to Adrienne, Chanel came to understand the power of mannequins. Soon her younger sister, Antoinette, was pressed into service.

2 Antoinette and Adrienne Chanel. Arm in arm and wearing creations taken from Gabrielle's boutique, the Chanel women promenaded along the pier at Deauville. And they always returned triumphant, trailing admirers who talked only of the ladies' stylishness. The shop was off to a splendid start.

SEM

the lady with the greyhound

The famed and feared caricaturist Sem was, if one can believe Jean Cocteau, "a ferocious insect, badly shaved, wrinkled, progressively taking on the tics of the victims he pursued. His fingers, his stump of a pencil, his round glasses, the onion-skin tracings that he tore up and superimposed, his forelock, his umbrella, his dwarfish, stable-boy silhouette—all seemed to shrink into and concentrate upon his eagerness to sting." Suddenly in 1913, Sem decided to aim at a new target: high fashion. The first fascicle in a series of albums entitled *Le Vrai et le Faux Chic* ("True and False Chic") appeared in March 1914, sowing panic throughout the fashion salons.

1   The lady with the greyhound was an example of "true" chic. And the woman seen by Sem as the very model of elegance was none other than For-sane, a famous *demi-mondaine*, whose fashion consultant proved to be Chanel. *Vrai chic* therefore represented the taste of Chanel.
2   The creators of *faux chic* had their new models presented to music and made the mannequins adopt grotesque hip-shot poses, all designed to seduce a clientele whose own demeanor and dress were of an extreme pomposity.

This merciless caricature won the great humorist many violent and long-lasting enmities.

an unexpected ally: Sem

1   A caricature by Sem sometimes had the effect of launching a career. This was the case when Sem drew Chanel in the arms of a centaur Boy Capel brandishing at the end of his polo mallet a *toque* in the latest fashion. The allusion could not be misconstrued: If Boy was Coco's lover, he was also the financial backer of her business. Chanel had the good sense to see the advantage of Sem's charge. And the caricaturist joined the ranks of her admirers.

2   Polo at Deauville, where Arthur Capel was top player. At the right Coco appears on horseback—with her collar open, which, seeming rather careless, created a scandal.

3   Goursat, or Sem, caricatured by himself.

true chic and false chic

Gabrielle Chanel became a young woman to 2 watch. But her celebrity was based on very little. Others might be famous by reason of their wealth or their extravagance. But about Chanel one simply said: "She is like nobody else." Her clients were neither those ranked by Sem among the victims of *faux chic* nor those "martyred by *couturiers* and mad milliners" who drove the great caricaturist to indignant comparisons: "Ah, what fools! Ah, what hats! Nothing has been omitted and nothing transformed—flower pots, lampshades, casseroles, every conceivable kind of lid. They tried everything and dared everything," Sem confided to *L'Illustration* in the March 28, 1914, issue.

1   Here, at the polo grounds in Deauville, Coco makes a face at Léon de Laborde, a member of the group of dandies without whom she was rarely seen. Once more Chanel stands apart from the crowd by virtue of the astonishing simplicity of her attire, an almost masculine tailleur made of white linen, completely unadorned by jewelry. No less spare is the hat, with its relatively discreet brim and its utter lack of "garnish." One can imagine the effect Coco had in town, dressed in such a radically new manner. And what can one think of Comte de Laborde's tweed cap? Worn at polo!
2   Two chairs away, a lady transports a good two pounds of muslin roses on her head, and on her bosom three cascading ropes of pearls.

Fashion also demanded that women endure shoes with pointed toes and triple straps that could be fastened only with the aid of a buttonhook. The talent of Gabrielle Chanel grew strong from swimming against the current.

tradition vs innovation

1 The year 1914 saw a beautiful June. And Chanel felt the moment had come for real change. With such scorching weather, it seemed possible that women might be persuaded to go bathing. Now, Coco borrowed the material of Boy's sweaters, an approach that she would often repeat in subsequent years, searching through the wardrobes of her lovers for elements of masculine attire. Thus was born a very chaste bathing suit.

1 Male bathers were the main attraction, but occasionally a female would venture into the water, always followed by disapproving looks given through lorgnettes. Among the daring swimmers, Gabrielle Chanel.
2 Chanel ready to swim in July 1914.

August 1914

War. Deauville empty. No more gay young people. All dispersed by the cruel winds of battle. At the Deauville racetrack, no one but old men and little boys dressed in huge *jean-barts* ("Buster Brown" hats) and knee britches. Also, a lone young woman. It is Gabrielle, from head to toe . . . Chanel. A photograph in the local press captured the image of this familiar habituée of the paddock, whose sartorial tastes went so utterly against the tendencies of the day. She wore a loosely fitting tailleur. But fashion, until then, had taken as its sole purpose the accentuation of women's physical charms—and that, sometimes, to the point of caricature. Create a suit that would eliminate the need for a corset? A garment under which the body was merely suggested? This is what Gabrielle dared. She was convinced that by cultivating the natural, she would not suppress femininity—quite the contrary. The reception women gave her work confirmed this. As the guns of August began to sound Chanel realized her first big commercial success as an *haute couturière*.

What would become of her in Deauville? Who would want couture at this time? Boy, now in uniform, counseled her to stay put and, above all, not to close her shop. On August 23, 1914, thanks to the German victory at the battle of Charleroi in Belgium, that advice assumed dramatic relevance. *Châtelains* with summer houses in Deauville sought refuge there, making the seaside resort during the war the aristocratic city it had been in time of peace. Women needed to be able to move about on foot, to walk rapidly, and without encumbrance. This made the Chanel outfit the dress of the moment. A veritable *salon* developed in the shade of the great awning protecting the entrance to the boutique of Gabrielle Chanel. The little milliner had become a commanding lady.

a dying world

War? In Deauville no one could believe it. Still, the distant reality did have an effect on the outward forms of local existence. The deliberate ostentation, the obligatory display of wealth, pleasure pursued as a duty—all that would be swept away.

In actuality, it was the onset, after a fourteen-year delay, of the final death agony of a stubbornly long-lived 19th century. But even this hardly seemed evident at Deauville. How can one believe that the world is really coming to an end? The end of the long afternoons spent making social calls, of taking tea at the polo grounds, of glorious entrances at the races, where women presented themselves—all sumptuousness and delicacy—wearing dresses whose maintenance was the despair of maids.

As Chanel would express it: "A world was dying, while another was being born. I was there, an opportunity came forward, and I took it. I was the same age as the new century, and it was to me that it looked for sartorial expression. . . . The paddock before '14! I had no doubt that while at the races, I was in attendance at the death of luxury, at the demise of the 19th century, and also at the end of an era."

In Paris, men left for the front singing: "Long live the tomb! Death is nothing."

the front was collapsing

August 1914 was the time of the invasion. German troops entered France at Saint-Quentin on the 27th, and on the 28th a dramatic communiqué informed the French people just how massive the attack had been: "From the Somme to the Vosges. . . ." Magnificent châteaux were destroyed: Tilleloy and Anisay burned and reduced to ashes. At Deauville appeared the beautiful people who had inhabited the palatial country houses, tearfully telling how "they had lost everything." And it was true. Still, they retained the means to reconstitute their wardrobes. This took them to the only boutique that had not closed its doors: *chez* Chanel.

In early September the Germans ceased to be *les allemands* and became *les boches*. Meanwhile, the French government abandoned Paris for Bordeaux. The front collapsed. At Deauville a new wave of refugees flowed in from yet more châteaux, mainly those in Seine-et-Oise. With the enemy forces only 30 kilometers away, Parisians were fleeing. This gave Deauville its last influx of the wealthy dispossessed. Chanel no longer knew where to seat her clients. What a curious fate that a Frenchwoman should owe the Germans the opportunity to improve her business and make herself known beyond anything that would have been possible in Paris.

1915: lovers at Biarritz

To whom did Boy Capel owe his transfer from the army to the Franco-English war-time coal commission? Clémenceau could not have been absent when the decision was made. It placed Boy in a world that few men of that time could even have imagined—far from the menace of the first warplanes, the assault of the first tanks, the whole battle zone. It returned him to Paris and London. But before taking up his new assignment, Boy carried Gabrielle off to the Côte Basque.

1916: a new silhouette

In wartime France one heard about those who suffered at the front, those in Paris who never ceased talking, and those at Biarritz who profited. The profiteers declared themselves eager to buy anything, by which they meant rather precisely: *le luxe*.

It occurred to both Boy and Gabrielle that in Biarritz they could repeat the experience of the year before at Deauville, along with all its happy results. Thus, a few days before his departure, Boy advanced the funds, and Gabrielle opened not a boutique but an actual *maison de couture* offering a collection of dresses priced at three-thousand francs each. Never had Biarritz seen a *couturière* so sumptuously installed—not in a shop but in a villa facing the casino. Chanel had her war plan. Biarritz, after all, was a sort of advanced position that put Spain within range. Neutrality and proximity made this country an excellent source of not only material but also wealthy clients. It gave the Biarritz enterprise a solid base. Gabrielle began in July and had everything in place by September. And she did not have to wait long to discover the value of her initiative. Orders flowed in, from the Spanish court, from Madrid, from San Sebastian, from Bilbao, etc. The Biarritz atelier was soon working at full capacity. At the end of the year, Gabrielle had achieved victory, virtually by herself, and was back in Paris. In complete command, she wanted personally to assure the liaison between her outposts. She supplied Biarritz directly, leaving her sister Antoinette in charge with full powers. In Paris, one of her ateliers worked only for Spanish clients. Now, like a general deploying his reserves according to the needs of war, Gabrielle recruited in Paris whatever personnel she lacked in Biarritz and, in a riskier manoeuvre, nagged Basque mothers into letting their daughters go to Paris, and this despite the zeppelins. Defeated, the mothers surrendered. Early in 1916 Gabrielle held sway over almost three-hundred employees. To her surprise, she found herself able to reimburse Boy Capel, which she did without even asking his opinion.

1 Boy and Gabrielle at Saint-Jean-de-Luz. With his back turned, the sugar magnate Constant Say.
2 Biarritz, where the war changed nothing and where the Hôtel du Palais retained its peaceful air. There couples danced every night, forgetting the bad times with the tango.
3 In a 1916 issue of *Harper's Bazaar* appeared the first Chanel design ever published: a dress from the Biarritz collection. Created for Antoinette's beautiful clients, it had immense allure without a trace of pre-war elaborateness.

Both structured bodice and high collar have been eliminated, and the garment, which is slit down the front as if by a saber, opens on a vest cut like a man's waistcoat. Instead of puffing out, the sleeves hug the arms like stockings. The hat is close-fitting and remains unburdened by the veils, plumes, and other accessories that formerly were the glory of women's headgear. As for the waist, it has disappeared, giving way to a scarf, softly slipped over the hips and left to float like a commander's sash.

Surprised, but nevertheless admiring, the American editors hailed this creation with a brief legend, calling it the "charming chemise dress" of Chanel. The *couturière* would wait four years before receiving such a consecration in the French press. It took until 1919–20 for the country to recover its taste for frivolity.

99

1917: Paris' permissive style

The *Gazette du bon ton* ceased publication in 1914. And the disappearance of all the journals that had made French fashions known abroad explains why the feat of walking and showing a bit more than the ankle would remain a Parisian exclusive until 1919. Only after World War I did the French become aware of the shock felt by foreign visitors when confronted with that fraction of visible leg. But hardly had the fashion been seen when it became universal.

In 1916 Chanel set out to find a machine-made fabric as close to knitting as possible. Rodier, in lieu of something better, showed her a material then considered unusable: jersey. But it proved to be precisely what Chanel wanted: knitting made by machine. She swore to Rodier that the fabric would take over the market.

1 Antoinette Chanel in Biarritz, during her "full powers" at Chanel's *maison de couture*.
2 A Chanel ensemble reproduced in the American *Vogue* in February 1917. The loosely belted jacket is made of jersey.
3 In March 1917 *Les Élégances parisiennes* made a full-page announcement of a new "fashion" fabric: jersey. Hats and dresses by Gabrielle Chanel.
4 In the same issue, three Chanel jacket-skirt ensembles made of jersey. *Les Élégances* was a publicity organ.
5 Hilda May on a motor scooter and in a Chanel.

Les Dernières Créations de la Mode

Les tissus de laine sont très souples. — Beaucoup de taffetas de fantaisie. — Le jersey est encore à la mode.

T voilà les nouveaux tissus! Les nouveaux chapeaux! Les nouvelles robes! Cet essaim de nouveautés, cet amas de surprises ensoleille pour nous les heures mornes de février. Il semble, à manier toutes ces robes nouvelles, ces foulards adorablement fleuris, que les beaux jours d'été soient proches, les beaux jours pendant lesquels nous ne serons pas "rationnés" de soleil... Et je vais parcourir joyeusement avec vous les gammes des tissus, depuis la gabardine jusqu'à l'organdi.

Tout est souple ou presque : les beaux lainages très fins et très légers tombent en plis moelleux,... un peu d'apparence veloutée, quelques étoffes *peignées,* d'un aspect très chaud sans l'être... Dans les domaines des soieries, nous retrouvons les véritables soies d'été, le joli foulard aux mille dessins, la toile de soie, le shantung, le satin souple et le taffetas. Ceci est une surprise apportée par les

nouveaux "paniers" que l'on essaie de relancer, ou tout au moins par les draperies des robes-tonneaux.

Et puis voici des linons, des crêpes imprimés, car nous sommes tout à *l'impression,* pour les soieries comme pour les lainages, et, naturellement, avant tout, à l'impression cachemire. Où ne trouvera-t-on pas ce dessin fameux, cette palme, ces coloris?... Dans une seule maison de tissus en coton, j'ai compté jusqu'à dix coloris de cachemire, du plus voyant au plus effacé. J'ai peur que nous ne nous lassions très vite de cette fantaisie qui tourne à l'obsession.

LES TISSUS DE LAINE

Chez Rodier, je veux, avant toute chose, vous mentionner leur triomphant *djersabure...* C'est un jersey plutôt épais, à grosses mailles, d'une apparence plutôt rugueuse ; mais quels beaux plis souples forme ce tissu! On l'apprécie fort chez tous les Couturiers et l'on en a fait des

◀ 169

COSTUMES DE JERSEY
Modèles de Gabrielle Chanel (*fig. 257, 258 et 259*)

PUISQUE LES TAXIS SONT RARES...

... Puisque l'essence nous est comptée, puisque les chauffeurs ne sont pas toujours aussi aimables qu'on le voudrait, il a fallu chercher un nouveau moyen de locomotion. La « patinette automobile », semblable à celle qui fait la joie des enfants, permet de ne plus dépendre d'un conducteur narquois qui consent à vous mener à la Bastille lorsque vous avez besoin d'aller à Passy. *L'exemple que nous donne ici Mlle Hilda May incitera-t-il les Parisiennes à adopter ce petit véhicule ?*

the feminine ankle

Gabrielle immediately adopted the new fabric—jersey—for herself. What she made with it—an unbelted, three-quarter-length overcoat, free of all ornament and almost masculine in its severity—dispelled the doubts of her suppliers.

But even a firm less alert than Rodier, without knowing anything at all, but responsive to what makes true feminine elegance, would have seen right away that this garment offered something highly original in its sheer freedom. Here, embellishment ceded to line, giving effect to a costume born of the single-minded logic of its creator. Chanel wanted to achieve what no one else had dared to do with such candor: women going forth liberated by shortened skirts and by loosely fitting garments that de-emphasized the bust and lower curves. Chanel imposed upon fashion a novelty so decisive that it literally brought clothing into the 20th century. As for the nostalgic ones—and there were many of them who, like Marcel Proust in *Du côté de chez Swann*, expressed sadness at the sight of dresses "not even made of material" and of "ordinary-looking" women—their laments would remain futile, for nothing could revive a defunct way of dressing.

1 May 1918. Gabrielle Chanel, lying in the fallow grass of a meadow, could be taken as a symbol of the year the war ended and of the discreet elegance of French women at this time. Moreover, her hat and her dress both conceal secrets: under the first, bobbed hair; under the second, no corset whatever.
2 Chanel standing, dressed in the same model.
3 Illustration in *Femina*, February 1917. An ensemble made of jersey, consisting of a three-quarter-length jacket and a loose skirt, typical of those launched by Chanel.
4 Coco Chanel playing golf at Saint-Jean-de-Luz. Success agrees with women, and it made Chanel still more beautiful. That year she had bought the Villa Larralde for her business, paying three hundred thousand francs cash. Everything worked for her, even in Paris during the worst year of the war, when the capital was menaced by a new cannon, whose bombardments brought the walls of Saint-Gervais down on the Good Friday congregation.
5 Dressed by Chanel, Adrienne and Antoinette at the races, accompanied by the Maharajah of Indore, who, of all the foreigners in the colony of allies, had the richest taste. Boutet de Monvel did his portrait, showing the Indian Prince full length wearing an ample black cape lined in white satin.

103

Chanel at Uriage,
in Basque beret and bobbed hair

1918 was the year the awful war reaccelerated, as if four years of fierce struggle had been for nothing. Once more the Germans advanced and disaster seemed imminent. With the enemy at the gates of Paris, the well-to-do fled anew to Deauville or to Biarritz. But atrocious as it was, this dramatic crisis did not prove a disservice to Gabrielle. As before, the war played right into her hands, for nothing could prevent its giving women what had always been beyond their reach: freedom.

The great novelty was that women no longer had to ask permission to go wherever they wished. The worldly ones even dared to enter the Ritz bar, where access had been denied them in time of peace. Located, as chance would have it, directly across the street was Chanel's boutique, at 21 Rue Cambon. Henceforth, Gabrielle would find herself on the route taken each day by women eager to know what moved and lived in a great city, where for the first time they were circulating alone and on foot.

1   A sporty woman in a Basque beret: Chanel. Five years earlier, two Englishwomen who on a windy day at Deauville had dared to adopt such a headdress found themselves accused of eccentricity.
2   In a man's sweater: Chanel again. Still innovative, she had just proved her independence by cutting her hair even shorter than in 1917. This too was quickly copied.
3   With their hair bobbed, Adrienne and Gabrielle looked more alike than ever.
4   A hiker in a style never seen before, carrying a cane and wearing a thick cardigan, an ample skirt, and a long scarf. Round-toed, white, and simple, the shoes—like the whole outfit—have something British about them, a quality absorbed from Boy.

1

the conversion to short hair

Bobbed hair was shocking, irreversible, and, on the whole, grudgingly accepted. Only by means of the most absurd ruses did women get their families to tolerate the new style. Thus Colette, in order to appease her in-laws, pretended that she had accidently overturned an oil lamp onto her loosened hair. But in sacrificing, at Willy's instigation, tresses measuring some 1.58 meters, she involuntarily anticipated fashion by at least a decade. This was in 1903, when, in the company of a similarly coiffed Polaire and an opera-hatted Willy, her appearance in a theatre box created a scandal, causing Willy to be known along the boulevards as "the man with two monkeys."

1   A coiffure adopted by Dorziat for her attendance at a gala performance of the Ballets Russes at the Châtelet. Published in 1912 in *Comoedia*, this photograph served to announce that "the Spanish shell comb and its derivatives are the rage, all graceful complements to supple waves." Three years later, the hair style would look a century old.

5

The bobbed-hair offensive got underway in May 1917, the date verified in the journal of Paul Morand: "For three days now the fashion has been for women to wear short hair. Everyone has adopted it, with Mme Letellier and Chanel leading the way. . . ."

2   Among the new converts to this fashion was Marthe Davelli, a talented and beautiful singer who had quickly gained stardom at the Opéra-Comique six years before. In Davelli, Gabrielle found not only a friend but also a veritable double. The two young women accentuated their resemblance by arranging their hair in the same way.

3   Gabrielle Chanel in 1917, the period in which Morand noted in his *Journal d'un attaché d'ambassade* that Coco "is definitely becoming a personage."

4   The only album of drawings by Modigliani that has survived intact contains among its twenty-seven sheets this 1915 portrait of Madame Kisling, who pioneered bangs.

5   Caryathis during the run of *La Belle Excentrique*, when she too became a devotée of the scandalous *coiffure à la Jeanne d'Arc*.

an unheard-of audacity: sunbathing

No one but street vendors and peasants had ever been tanned. Whereas a milky skin seemed a sure sign of aristocracy, a tanned one could indicate nothing but modest or plebeian origins. This attitude had long been in effect, and, among all the innovations undertaken by Chanel, the idea of fearing the sun less would prove to be the most difficult to promote. It was not until 1923 that women could be seen on the beach sunning themselves without even a hat for protection. Here, in 1918, a bareheaded Chanel blissfully drinks in the sun's rays while a more reticent Adrienne still wears a hat. But it is revealing to note that even though Chanel dared to let the sun have its way with her face, she continued to cover her hands. Gloves were essential because sun-darkened hands suffered still more negative prejudice than a tanned face. Neither in public nor in private could a woman of the world risk having her hands look as if they had done manual labor.

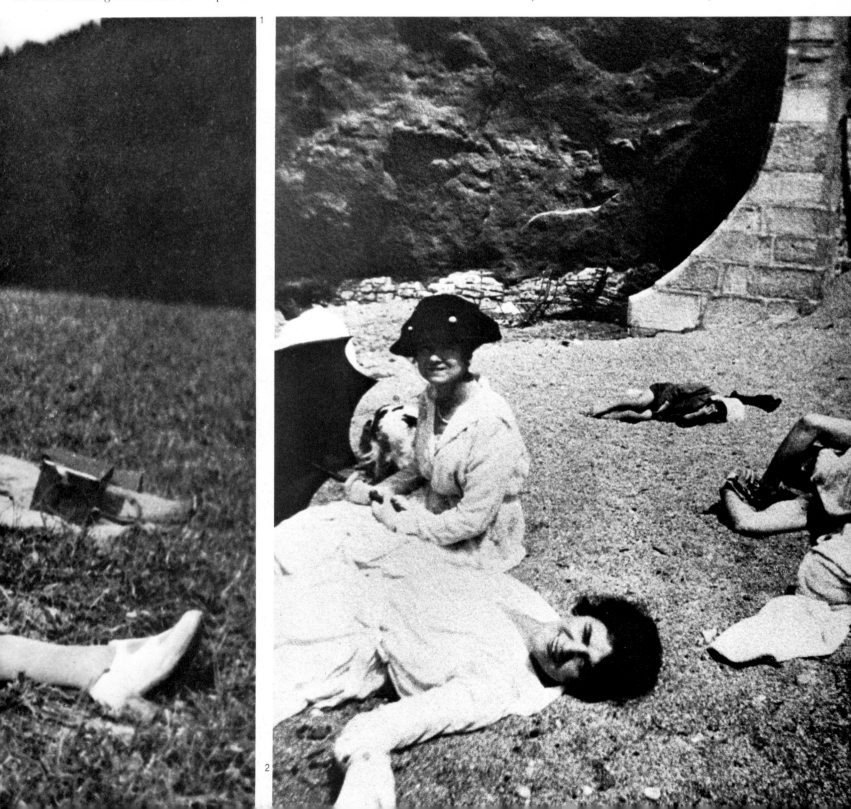

1

2

comfort: an intoxicating freedom

If feminine fashion remained beholden to Poiret for such important innovations as the softening of the corset and a slight abridgment of skirts, and if Poiret was a colorist unlike anyone who came after him, it was nonetheless Gabrielle who in 1918 insisted on the right of women to comfort and ease of movement. Everything favored it. The notion of woman as an object or possession could exist no longer, and the victory of the automobile over horse-drawn carriages was an accomplished fact, bringing about a whole new conception of how to clothe the female body. "I set the fashion for a quarter of a century," said Chanel. "Why? Because I knew how to express my own time."

1   Gabrielle, Arthur Capel's automobile, and Marguerite Vincent. Formerly a dancer at the Monnaie in Brussels, this friend from the Moulins days had now succeeded Maud Mazuel as chaperone and companion to Adrienne Chanel.

1

Poiret had created a fluid style, without a cinched waist. Chanel went further and left the waist scarcely indicated. Poiret allowed the foot to appear, but Gabrielle emphasized the skirt's rise by generously freeing the ankle. In the same stroke she also eliminated the need for a certain movement that men had so voluptuously ogled: the gesture used by women to gather up their skirts in preparation for mounting a step. What else disappeared? An era in the life of women, their demands as clients to whom everything was owed; the exclusivity of fabrics and designs. Until then, it would have been the ruin of a *couturier* should a customer encounter another woman wearing a similar creation. In changing all that, Chanel transformed forever the whole appearance of street life.

2   Chanel on vacation in 1918.
3   From left to right: Gabrielle, Marguerite Vincent, and Adrienne Chanel, all wearing the same Chanel model.

Misia, her husbands, her painters, her musicians, her poets

It was at a dinner in the home of Cécile Sorel, in 1917, that Gabrielle Chanel first met the only woman who ever had an undeniable (though unacknowledged) influence upon her—the only woman in fact to whom Chanel would grant any genius whatever.

Misia Sophie Olga Zénaïde Godebska had been born in March 1872 in, quite by accident, St. Petersburg. Her father was Polish and her mother half-Russian and half-Belgian. Even though pregnant, Madame Godebska decided to join her sculptor-painter husband in Russia, where she knew he could not be trusted among women. Having successfully surprised him installed with a mistress, she gave birth to a daughter and then died.

This left Misia to be brought up by her Russian grandmother, a spendthrift musician, and her grandfather, a violin virtuoso who taught the infant notes before she could learn the alphabet. Several stepmothers, some more sympathetic and some less, succeeded one another until one day Misia's father decided to claim his daughter.

Together, they lived in several different Parisian houses, which, depending upon Godebski's success or lack of it, could be either modest or sumptuous. Misia detested all of them and never ceased to miss the pseudo-Italian villa of her beloved grandmother. Located in the outskirts of Brussels, it was a house that simply vibrated with music, where a consumptive pianist died at the keyboard while playing Chopin, and where Liszt had come as a friend, taking a tiny Misia on his knee to play her Beethoven's Bagatelle in E-flat.

Placed in a boarding school at the Sacré-Coeur, Misia remained there six years, wildly impatient for the great day each week when she went for her piano lesson with Fauré.

At age fifteen, during summer vacation, Misia had a violent altercation with one of her stepmothers and fled to London, where, with four thousand francs borrowed from the Portuguese Consul, she set up alone. That at least is the version she gave of what has remained a rather mysterious escapade. Some months later, however, Misia was back in Paris with a place in a modest lodging. She lived from piano lessons procured for her by Fauré. Holding his pupil in highest esteem, the great composer predicted a career for her on the concert stage.

When he learned of her engagement, Fauré dissolved into tears. Misia nonetheless married a cousin, Thadée Natanson, who was Polish-born but had become French. He was twenty, she twenty-one years old. Even though admitted to the bar, Natanson spent less time there than in artistic and literary circles. Proust, Monet, Renoir, Odilon Redon, Signac, Debussy, Mallarmé, Gide, and, most of all, the Nabis and Toulouse-Lautrec, with whom Thadée had especially strong ties, became the habitués of the young couple's salon in Rue Saint-Florentin. All the guests of that house were, without exception, sensitive to the youth, the pianistic gifts, and the charm of Misia, whose image her painter-friends recorded with an astonishing variety and abundance.

1, 2 Two portraits of Misia executed by Vuillard around 1896–97, when Misia was about twenty-five.

Misia and
La Revue blanche

It was in 1889 at Spa that a group of young vacationers, among them Alexandre and Thadée Natanson, decided to found a review for the purpose of advancing new talent and ideas. What emerged was the famous *Revue blanche*, which Gide called *le centre de toutes les divergences*. While Alexandre served as director, Thadée became editor and indeed the main driving force behind the whole enterprise. After starting in Belgium, it soon moved to Paris. Proust, Barrès, Verlaine, Fénéon, Zola, Mallarmé, Jarry, Léon Blum, Oscar Wilde, Francis Jammes, Mirbeau, Claudel, and Péguy all appeared in a journal that for twelve years came out monthly or bi-monthly and had a decisive influence on the arts and letters of the period.

Posters promoting *La Revue blanche* were created by Thadée's friends, Toulouse-Lautrec, Vuillard, and Bonnard, all of whom took the editor's young wife as their favorite model. Thus, Misia, whether dressed in a high-collared black coat or in a fur wrap, muff, and veil, came to symbolize *La Revue blanche* in the eyes of the French intelligentsia.

1 A rare photograph of Misia Natanson wearing a coat with triple *pèlerine*.
2 Bonnard, *La Revue blanche* poster. Misia in her triple cape.
3 Toulouse-Lautrec, *La Revue blanche* poster. Misia with her muff.

the beautiful Madame Edwards

"Thadée was becoming more and more preoccupied with finances," wrote Misia in her memoirs, adding: *"La Revue blanche* had heavy expenses, and year by year the deficit became more difficult to cover." Thadée needed a Maecenas, for he himself was more than half-ruined. When the benefactor appeared, he was Alfred Edwards, the newspaper magnate and founder of *Le Matin,* which had the largest circulation in France. Now the charm of Misia had its predictable effect upon Edwards, who lost no time in "saving" the husband by separating him from his wife.

Edwards had been born in Pera, the European quarter in Constantinople, of a father who, as physician to the Sultan's harem, had accumulated a considerable fortune. Although horribly jealous—"the jealousy of a Turk," said Misia—Edwards managed to agree that Misia should continue to see her painter-friends. It was in her beautiful apartment on the Rue de Rivoli that Misia posed for the nearly paralyzed Renoir, whose large portrait shows his subject dressed in pink. It was also here, in the little salon "hung with green silk and illuminated by two windows overlooking the Tuileries," that Bonnard—with his sweet, myopic expression, dumbfounded by all the luxury—painted the celebrated portrait reproduced below.

But cordiality between Misia and Edwards did not last long. It dissolved when he left her for a beautiful *demi-mondaine:* Lanthelme. This new relationship, however, had a tragic and mysterious end: Lanthelme, from the bridge of Edwards' yacht, jumped into the Rhine. The affair did great damage to Edwards, and in 1909 he and Misia were divorced.

1 Bonnard, *Misia,* 1908–09.

2 Misia in 1908, followed by her husband, Alfred Edwards, the owner of *Le Matin* and the principal shareholder in *Le Figaro.* "I was among the first to own one of those engines born of the brains of Messieurs de Dion, Bouton, Panhard, and Levassor, which could achieve a speed of 30 kilometers per hour," wrote Misia proudly in her memoirs, published posthumously in 1952. "It was not without a slight shudder that one climbed upon the fold-out runningboard so as to wedge oneself into the upholstered seats."

A few years later, Maillol wanted her to pose for him. "Beauty should be copied wherever it is found," he wrote to her. "Quite naturally, therefore, I address myself to you." The sculptor saw her as an immortal figure, but she refused.

the great Misia Sert

If the second marriage of Misia Godebska developed her taste for luxury, it was a third union, in 1914, this time with the bearded Catalan painter José-Maria Sert, that marked the beginning of her public fame. From that time forward, no artistic manifestation occurred without the involvement of the influential Misia. The friend of Diaghilev, of the dancers he promoted, of the choreographers, designers, and musicians he discovered, Misia became associated with every one of the impresario's creations. What a destiny! This inspirational force, this counselor who

for fifty years lived among the greatest artists of her time, making herself indispensable to them, actually was a person of no culture whatever. "She never opened a book," said Chanel. "She does not even read her mail!" Which was true.

1 Vuillard, *Misia Sert*, 1915.
2 Jean Cocteau, drawing of Misia at Monte Carlo in 1911, at the time of the first performance of the ballet *Spectre de la rose*. With her are José-Maria Sert, Jean Cocteau, and Sergei de Diaghilev.

the tragic sport of automobiles

The year 1919 marked the renewal of the sport of automobile driving after the interruption caused by World War I. Although the lack of materials was cruelly felt, racing recommenced with the professional drivers, many of them now fighter-plane veterans, redoubling their daring. This was certainly true of the famous "Rick"—Rickenbaker, the American "ace" of the French flying forces—and André Boillot, who in 1919 won the dangerous *Targa Florio* in Sicily. That year, 21 contestants made their start in abominable weather and along roads that had been transformed into sloughs. The test, consisting of 4 times around 1,500 turns and over a mountainous circuit 800 kilometers long, produced a brutal contest. The press remarked on the "mad temerity" of Boillot who, pushed by Ascaria, brushed precipes, scraped rocks, ground down masses of stone, and skidded over mountain snows. Ascari, just when he had broken the record for this course, disappeared into a ravine. As for Boillot, he was in sight of the goal when some spectators surged onto the roadway, protesting the victory of a foreigner. Boillot had no choice but to slam on the brakes, and after a triple spin, he finally crossed the finish line—backwards! The spirited presence of the American journalist W.F. Bradley, a passionate admirer of French pilots and airplane builders, saved Boillot from disqualification. Bradley quickly implored the French driver to restart his motor and to make a second pass over the line, this time front first. Exhausted, Boillot complied, with the jeers of the mob ringing in his ears. Shouting *C'est pour la France*! he fainted. Just then two Italians arrived—Gambori and Mariando—but it was too late. The unconscious Boillot was declared the winner. His race, now a legend in Sicily, has remained one of the most extraordinary feats in the annals of the automobile.

The year 1919 was also when touring by automobile caught on, especially among the affluent who could afford a chauffeur. Boy Capel became one of the first victims among those said to be afflicted by a "contagious madness." The handsome Boy was killed on December 24 of that year. A news agency dispatch gave the facts: "Captain Capel was traveling from Paris. He was on his way to Cannes when a tire on his automobile blew out." With the death of Boy, the killer car cut a bloody path into high society. The tragic event left Chanel broken and, for once, incapable of masking the immense sorrow that she felt. She was, in fact, mourning Boy for the second time, the first having occurred in 1918, when, for reasons of his own personal ambition, he married Lady Diana Wyndham, which made him the brother-in-law of Lord Lovat. It was Chanel's friends José-Maria and Misia Sert who undertook to restore her will to live.

This brought Gabrielle into the circle of artists where Misia reigned. Now the *couturière* gained the authority that allowed her, in subsequent years, to appreciate and defend talents that were as diverse as they were original.

1 Spring 1919, Gabrielle Chanel en route to Biarritz.
2 A bad accident in the south of France.

Avec stupeur, j'appris de la bouche de Bienvenu,
Que les obus peuvent fleurir sans l'aide de cette bienfaisante
pluie: la musique patriotique.
(Moi, qui sais de la guerre ce qu'en sait . un habitué
des cinémas!)

aid for a child

Raymond Radiguet belonged to the generation that had been deprived of its fathers by the war but that had not itself endured the hell of the trenches. Radiguet's precocity as well as his rage to live aroused both fear and indignation. Max Jacob, who had discovered Radiguet in 1918 and had introduced him to Cocteau and then to Misia, described the youth: "He was handsome, he was grave. He had, it seemed, read everything. He was imperturbable. He could be seen almost every night sitting at the Boeuf sur le Toit. Radiguet drank a considerable amount, but his face, his heavy mouth, his stubborn eyebrows remained absolutely immobile." It should be recalled that he was hardly fourteen years old when he wrote his first poem, "*Les Joues en feu*"; that he was seventeen when his masterpiece, *Le Diable au corps*, transformed this *enfant terrible* into a monster in the eyes of those whom the novel scandalized. It must also not be forgotten that he died

of the century: Radiguet

while only twenty, of a badly treated typhoid infection, after having completed *Le Bal du comte d'Orgel*, which came out two weeks after the author's death. Finally, we should remind ourselves that it was Chanel whom Cocteau called when it became necessary to transport the fever-racked Radiguet from his hotel room to a Paris hospital. She paid all the medical bills.

1 Roger de La Fresnaye, drawing of Raymond Radiguet, April 1921.
2 Manuscript by Raymond Radiguet entitled *In Memoriam*, written c.1919. He was then sixteen years old.
3 Vacation at Pramousquier in 1922. P. de Lacretelle, Radiguet, Jean Hugo, Georges Auric, Valentine Hugo, and the official pianist of the Groupe des Six, Marcelle Meyer.
4 Jean Oberlé, drawing of Radiguet with his discoverer and promoter: Jean Cocteau.

121

Paris, where nothing was as before

The world of Marcel Proust is dead, and we are in the time of Radiguet. Just as fashionable events changed in spirit, so the *grands seigneurs* changed their style, and the great *locomotives* of the Belle Époque lost out in their hope of reviving the prewar days when members of a class could associate only with one another.

The turn-of-the-century era belonged to Comte Boni de Castellane, with his Palais Rose imitating Versailles, his extraordinary *fêtes*, and his frigid formality.

And 1920? It was the time of Comte Étienne de Beaumont. At his townhouse *le monde*—meaning the only "world" that counted, that of the aristocracy—mingled for the first time with exponents of nonofficial, nonacademic, un-"honored" art. Beaumont became the inventor of a new form of snobbism requiring that value take precedence over title, talent over wealth, artists over the establishment. In Beaumont's gilded *boiserie* salon, bordering on the Rue Masseran, Proust attended the last *soirée* of his life. He was received like a sovereign. Later, whole troupes of timid young unknowns—painters, musicians, writers, poets—made themselves known and got their start in the home of Étienne de Beaumont. But the true Beaumont, who could claim to have unmasked *him*? Under an exterior of grandiose frivolity, he hid a lacerated sensibility. His style also provoked a good bit of ridicule, but the Count saw no other way of expressing his horror of sensible behavior. For those of facile judgment and hasty comment, the name of the Comte de Beaumont signifies little more than an elegant manner and a lingering memory of receptions, balls, and parties of exceptional liveliness and fantasy. Happily, there are other observers.

For them, Beaumont remains the sole French aristocrat—with the possible exception of the Vicomte de Noailles—who supported the new spirit, the only one whose involvement was not limited simply to encouragement. In creating *Les Soirées de Paris* Beaumont was, in the

course of a brief season (May–June 1924), the organizer of truly astonishing spectacles that must be counted among the most stimulating of their time. Although irritating to the lovers of traditional ballet, the creations of *Les Soirées de Paris* consisted of both danced pantomime and *tableaux vivants*, whether the individual work was Cocteau and Jean Hugo's *Roméo et Juliette* or *Mercure* ("plastic poses" in three scenes by Massine, Satie, and Picasso.

The eroticism of *Mercure* and Picasso's "found objects" provoked vigorous protests from the public. But Diaghilev—even though uninvited and disturbed by Beaumont's undertaking, which he saw as a possible threat to himself—attended that evening and loudly expressed his enthusiasm.

A commission from Étienne de Beaumont for *Les Soirées de Paris* gave Marie Laurencin the opportunity to create the sets and costumes used in the ballet *Les Roses*.

1 Marie Laurencin (on the right), whose art now seems so childish—"Ladies' work," said Forain contemptuously, "a stitcher of shoes"—but who will forever seem sacred for having been the great passion of Apollinaire. Here she is with Nicole Groult, then a famous *couturière* and the wife of André Groult whose furniture designs typified the 1920s to perfection.
2 The Comte de Beaumont's love of charades and *tableaux vivants* became the fashion. Every party in Paris served as an occasion for spectacle. Here, at the home of the Prince de Lucinge, are the actor and producer Marcel Herrand with Comtesse de Beaumont and Chanel done up as a fakir!
3 The Comte de Beaumont, as portrayed by Picasso. Beaumont, as much as his wife, had fascinated Radiguet, who made this very Parisian couple the main characters in his novel *Le Bal du comte d'Orgel*, which appeared in 1923. In 1924 Gabrielle Chanel engaged Beaumont as director of design for her new line of jewelry.

Biarritz filled with émigrés

Tsarist Russia had completely foundered. Biarritz, meanwhile, was the rendezvous for those Romanovs who, after escaping the massacre, found refuge in France. Here, Marthe Davelli, the beautiful opera singer, introduced her friend Chanel to the Grand Duke Dmitri Pavlovitch. Twenty-one years old, he was a bachelor and a very handsome man. His presence on the historic night in January 1917 when the monk Rasputin was assassinated had endowed him with a certain mystery. It made him seem a Lorenzaccio, like de Musset's hero, which he was not.

1 Grand Duke Dmitri in 1914, as Lieutenant in the Guards Regiment.
2 Chanel in 1920 at Biarritz during her brief liaison with Grand Duke Dmitri, who was eleven years her junior. They became inseparable for a year, and remained loyal friends thereafter.

2

Slavic charm

"Princes of the blood have always filled me with immense pity. Their *métier*, when they practice it, is the saddest thing possible, and still sadder when they don't practice it," Chanel said to Morand in 1919. And Dmitri, it is true, had experienced an extremely sad childhood. His mother, Alexandra of Greece, died just after he was born. Then, his father, Grand Duke Paul, married a divorcée, which caused him to be banished by his cousin the Tsar and thus separated from his two children. At age eleven, Dmitri and his sister were placed with their Uncle Sergei, the governor of Moscow, and his wife, the Tsaritsa's deeply religious sister. In reality, Grand Duke Dmitri was brought up by nurses.

Chanel was quicker than anyone to understand Dmitri's singular form of misery, which was to grow up without a mother. But what fascinated her about this Prince was his innate sense of luxury. She succumbed to Slavic charm.

1 1894: Tea in the garden at Ilinskoie, the home of Grand Duke Sergei. Dmitri and his sister, under the supervision of nanny Fry and the assistant nurse, Miss Grove. One of the valets, Piotr, followed Dmitri into exile and lived with him at Chanel's home in Garches.

2 Family vacation at Ilinskoie. The Tsaritsa holds her first-born, Olga, on her knees. The Tsar is seated at her feet. Dmitri is the little boy with the sad face, wearing a large, wide-brimmed *jean-bart* ("Buster Brown") hat.

3 Dmitri and Marie in Moscow in 1904.

4 Efrimov, watercolor portrait of Dmitri. At age fourteen he was already an officer in the Second Regiment of Riflemen, called "the Royal Family," but here he wears the dress uniform of the Horse Guards.

5 In 1920 Chanel made a timid use of embroidery, which *Vogue* applauded.

6 A great event in the career of Chanel occurred in 1920 when she launched *Numéro 5*, presented in a spare, minimal bottle—a flagon as clean as a cube—that stood in stark contrast to the frippery then favored by perfumers. *Numéro 5* was a mixture of 128 ingredients, blended by an eminent chemist, Ernest Beaux, whose father had been employed at the Tsarist court.

7 1915: Seventeen months before the abdication of Nicholas II, Grand Duke Dmitri—seen here with the Tsarevitch Alexei—is aide-de-camp to the Tsar.

Lui Plairai–je ainsi ?

ROBE DU SOIR DE CHANEL

Chanel reste fidèle à elle-même et choisit cette robe pour représenter sa conception de la mode du soir aux lectrices de " Vogue ". Elle est en crêpe de Chine citron givré d'une broderie de strass. Sur chaque épaule une légère draperie donne l'illusion de manches et, flottant gracieusement pendant la danse, forme de petites ailes. Chacun croit apercevoir un ange, mais naturellement ce n'est pas une illusion cette fois, puisque c'est d'une jolie femme qu'il s'agit, n'est-ce pas Messieurs ?

rendezvous
at Garches, 1920–23

Chanel invited the Grand Duke Dmitri and his valet Piotr to Garches, where she had acquired a villa. The playwright Henri Bernstein, who first captivated the *boulevard* public in 1903, was her neighbor and also one of her numerous admirers.

1 The summer of 1920 in Garches. Chanel in a "sports cape," with the Bernsteins' little daughter. Beginning in this period, Chanel was regarded as the creator of "sports" fashion in France, and the press coverage she received grew more serious every day.

2 Chanel recruited embroiderers, thereby surprising the fashion world. Would she abjure what Poiret called her *misérabilisme de luxe* ("poverty de luxe")? In 1923 *Vogue* made note of "motifs borrowed from old Russian embroidery." Thus, even in her work, Chanel succumbed to Slavic charm, for her lovers' past always proved to be a source of rich inspiration.

3 The cape of the American YMCA volunteers prompted Chanel to create the "sports" cape that she featured in her 1920 collection and here wore in the streets of Garches.

4 Olga Thomas, drawing in *Vogue*, November 1920. Chanel tunic and skirt ensemble embroidered with the chain-stitching typical of her Russian period. Two chiffon panels fixed to the waist fall to points.

5 Dmitri spent his childhood putting on a succession of marvelous military uniforms. Here, at age eleven, he wears the eagle-crowned helmet of the Imperial Guard.

6 Marthe Davelli, who introduced Chanel to Grand Duke Dmitri, was the best friend of both. In 1923, at the peak of her career, she sang Massenet's *Grisélidis* at the Paris Opéra.

7 Illustration in *Vogue*, 1920. Chanel's evening cape.

8 Already a fake Chanel! Photographed at the races by the Seeberger brothers, 1923.

9, 10 Illustrations in *Vogue*, 1920. Two views of Chanel's mock-crinoline, a miracle of lightness. *Vogue:* "Chanel can do anything."

11 Adrienne, like a living advertisement for her niece Gabrielle's ideas, wore Chanel's hats as soon as they were created—even though as a resident of the provinces she still hesitated to shorten her skirts as drastically as they did in Paris.

12 Olga Thomas, drawing in *Vogue*, 1920. The little *tricorne* ("three-cornered hat"), a Chanel success in the 1920s.

La forme restant simple, l'originalité d'une toilette réside le plus souvent dans la garniture ; aussi les broderies sont elles plus que jamais en honneur. A côté des dessins modernes aux lignes exubérantes, nos robes et nos jaquettes reproduisent des motifs empruntés aux anciennes broderies russes et roumaines, et leurs couleurs mettent une jolie note éclatante sur le blanc et les teintes neutres des lainages. La Tchéco-Slovaquie nous a envoyé certaine décoration de blouses paysannes, aux tonalités très riches, et Chanel est allée jusqu'en Chine et aux Indes chercher l'inspiration des broderies compliquées dont elle recouvre ses manteaux. Quelques couturières reproduisent même des décorations d'anciennes poteries persanes mais il est évident que, comme ailleurs, l'originalité à outrance ne doit pas être recherchée au détriment du bon goût, et la sobriété sied au costume de campagne.

Une veste de Chanel, douce idée de crêpe beige, est ornée d'une broderie chenille de deux couleurs brun et jau...

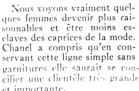

Nous voyons vraiment quelques femmes devenir plus raisonnables et être moins esclaves des caprices de la mode. Chanel a compris qu'en conservant cette ligne simple sans garnitures elle saurait se concilier une clientèle très grande et importante.

Quoi de plus simple que cette petite cape du soir dessinée (page 6) en crêpe de Chine noir, simplement retenue dans une bande étroite de fourrure grise qui va d'une épaule à l'autre ? Ce crêpe est monté à plat devant et derrière et marque simplement sur les côtés quelques larges plis qui tombent naturellement. On peut difficilement obtenir un résultat plus parfait avec un point de départ aussi simple.

Pour montrer que Chanel peut tout, voici un essai de la robe crinoline (page 6). Une robe à cerceaux dans le tulle noir le plus fin posé sur un fond étroit de crêpe de Chine. Pour toute garniture un ruban qui part des épaules et flotte librement.

Toutes les Parisiennes voudront avoir cette cape de Chanel si simple, en lourd crêpe de Chine noir, monté à plis sur une étroite bande de fourrure grise.

Chez Gabrielle Chanel le costume composé d'une robe et d'un manteau n'a rien perdu de ses faveurs. L'ensemble que voici est formé d'un corsage de crêpe broché blanc identique à la doublure du vêtement qui est droit, garni d'un empiècement prenant les épaules comme sur les versos; le plus nouveau est bizarre. La silhouette reste mince cependant; la draperie des côtés de la jupe est une concession à l'ampleur proposée actuellement, mais à laquelle Chanel n'est pas favorable. Une garniture d'hermine complète le vêtement au col et au bas des manches.

Chanel a si bien reconnu l'..on fine broderie exécutée au ...ns de chaînette, en fil de ...e gr clair et beige, tout le haut de ce manteau qu'il est très diffi.. ... reconnaître le crèpe m...

CHEZ CHANEL

LA PARISIENNE DE BON GOUT EST DAN

Tout ce qui, à Paris, s'intéresse à l'élégance, passe dans les salons de Chanel, et c'est un plaisir pour les yeux que ces réunions de jeunes femmes dont la toilette est étudiée jusqu'au moindre détail. Trois mannequins ondulent au milieu du salon : celui de gauche montre un manteau en lamé rose et argent garni de chinchilla imitation. Au centre est un costume en laine tricotée et kasha beige. La robe à trois volants est en Georgette noir, avec petite cape

1923–24: Chanel in her Russian phase

Imagine a more singular liaison than that of Gabrielle Chanel with the Grand Duke Dmitri Pavlovitch? She, the daughter of a fairground peddler who, somewhere in France, was still hawking suspenders and handkerchiefs from his pushcart at "2 francs a dozen"; he, the grandson of Alexander II, nephew of Alexander III, cousin of the last Tsar, who treated him as his own son, probably because the Tsarevitch had such precarious, even threatened health.

WOODRUFF

ÉLÉMENT

1 Alexei, the Tsarevitch, in uniform, next to the imperial train. He wears the belted blouse of the Russian infantry. 1916.

2 Illustration of a Chanel in *Vogue*, 1922. A blouse in kasha-colored khaki, with a skirt buttoned on the side. The sole ornament, a brown leather belt. Obviously, Russia had entered the designer's life.

3 Her embroidered dresses were so successful that Chanel had to create a workshop devoted to embroidery. The *directrice*? Grand Duchess Marie, Dmitri's sister, seen here.

4 Reinaldo Luza, drawing in *Vogue*, 1922. Chanel introduced the *roubachka*, the long belted blouse of the muzhiks (Russian peasants), now the uniform of Parisiennes. Here, with square *décolletage*, it is made of black crêpe-de-chine.

5 Pretty émigrées, all impoverished and uprooted, took jobs at Chanel's, where the *vendeuses* and the mannequins spoke Russian to one another. But discipline was strict. Jokingly, the ladies declared: "Only Freedericksz is missing!" This was the minister of the imperial household, an object of aversion on the part of noble white Russians, who scorned the "Baltic barons." Even the Tsar feared him, viewing

the old man as obsessed with protocol and calling him *le terrible moustache*. Here is Count Freedericksz in 1916.

6 Illustration in *Vogue*, 1922. An embroidered coat by Chanel.

7 Woodruff, drawing in *Vogue*, 1923. Never would so many fur coats and fur linings be seen at Chanel's as in these years.

8 The upholstered salon of the Russian imperial train in 1916. Left to right: Grand Duke Dmitri Pavlovitch, aide-de-camp to the Tsar; the Tsar and Tsaritsa; Grand Duke Mikhail Alexandrovitch, the Tsar's youngest brother in whose favor Nicholas II would abdicate a few months later; and finally the Grand Duchesses: Tatiana, Olga, Anastasia, and Marie. With the exception of Dmitri, all would perish by brutal assassination. The somewhat unsteady photograph was made by the Tsarevitch.

9 Sketch in *Vogue*, 1923. At Deauville there was a show of Chanel furs modeled by Russian ladies, who wore them with such ease that the rich garments seemed like everyday clothes. Whenever the mannequins encountered Dmitri, they called him "Your Majesty" and kissed his hand, to the great astonishment of the French public.

Chanel

Montparnasse replaces Montmartre

If Cubism was born in Montmartre, it was in Montparnasse that it matured and spawned movements that still animate the art of our time. Nothing could have been more different from the Montmartre Bohemia than the culture that replaced it. But no actual break occurred between these two cradles, far from it. What could not be tolerated, as Cocteau would remark, was going off the chosen route: "The Cubist code prohibited every journey except the north-south one, between the Place des Abbesses and the Boulevard Raspail."

In reality, it was in the period immediately preceding the Great War that this shift took effect, for in *Paris-Journal* appeared an article signed by Guillaume Apollinaire announcing that "the daubers no longer feel at home in modern Montmartre, now full of phony artists, commercial fantasists, and happy opium smokers. The real artists, meanwhile, are to be found in Montparnasse, all dressed like Americans." This would become more evident in 1917, with the ballet *Parade*. At the height of the war emerged the tendencies that, following the Armistice, would establish the tone and preeminence of those immense rendezvous for foreigners.

left to right Ortiz de Zarate, the Chilean painter whom Apollinaire called "the only Patagonian in Paris," and who stood by Modigliani in his last days; Max Jacob, the Breton Jew who the year before had been baptized, with Picasso as his godfather; Kisling the Pole, an incorrigible reveler; and Picasso the Spaniard, whose cap permits us to place the photo in time as accurately as if Picasso had dated it himself: 1917, the year of *Parade*.

The sole woman in the group is Paquerette, a conquest of Picasso's and one of those ineluctable figures always to be found at cafés where artists hang out. Location: La Rotonde.

Chanel goes Greek

This headline contained an element of surprise, since it did not concern fashion and appeared on the theatre page. Chanel was collaborating with artists who ten years later would make the informed public come running, but who at this time—1923—had yet to make their mark.

Antigone, in a free adaptation by Cocteau, with sets by Picasso, music by Honegger, and costumes by Chanel—this was the announcement posted at the Atelier, the theatre that Charles Dullin had just taken over and would direct for the next twenty years. Dullin and Chanel had known one another since about 1916, when he shared life with Caryathis high up on Montmartre in the studio where Chanel took her classes in eurythmic dance. Because of this old friendship, one can surmise that it was thanks as much to the demanding director of the Atelier as to Cocteau himself that Chanel received her first opportunity in the theatre.

This *Antigone*, in the opinion of some, would prove to be little more than a fatuous distraction for a few aesthetes, since those responsible for the production had limited or nonexistent knowledge of the classical theatre. Chanel, for instance, had never done a theatrical costume

in her life. As for Picasso, not to mention Cocteau, what could he make of Sophocles, having until then designed sets for nothing but light-hearted ballets?

1 A Greek actress, Genica Atanasiou, was an Antigone with close-cropped hair, plucked eyebrows, and eyes outlined in black and drawn towards the temples.
2 Georges Lapape, drawings commissioned by the French edition of *Vogue* as illustrations for an article devoted to Cocteau's *Antigone*. The piece appeared in February 1923.

with Cocteau, Picasso, and Chanel

Rave notices in the foreign press, which had no or almost no counterpart in Paris. The new style of *Antigone* baffled the critics, despite the clarifications that Cocteau fed to the journalists: "The characters in *Antigone* do not explain themselves. They act. They represent the kind of theatre that must replace the theatre of chit-chat." But it was the theatre of chit-chat—it was Sacha Guitry—that the Parisian public liked. And the Cocteau production— with its antique masks clustered about a loudspeaker serving as a choir, its actresses made up in white, its actors made up in red, and Antonin Artaud (who played Tiresias and in real life was Atanasiou's lover) reaching paroxysms of fury in his imprecations—left audiences dumbfounded.

a very provocative Antigone

1 Chanel's costume for Antigone: a large, heavy cape of brown wool.

2 Antigone between her two guards. The press compared Picasso's masks, grouped about a loudspeaker and the black shields with motifs taken from Delphi to store windows during Mardi Gras. Only the costumes by Chanel found favor: "These woolen clothes in neutral tones look like antique garments rediscovered after centuries," said *Vogue*. Meanwhile, Cocteau declared: "I ordered costumes from Chanel because she is the greatest *couturière* of our time."

3 Chanel's costumes for Hemon and Creon. Dullin played Creon as a tyrant "drunk with rage and stupid power," said Cocteau.

4 Belted about Dullin's head is a rather barbaric-looking band, probably the first piece of jewelry to come from the hands of Gabrielle Chanel.

Meyer, who wrote the article, counted for more than mere publicity: it amounted to a consecration. This was true, first of all, because of the Baron's exalted social standing. Of German nationality, he was simply Demeyer Watson before gaining a title by virtue of his marriage to a natural daughter of Edward VII. In addition, De Meyer had become a peerless photographer. The grace and Whistlerian style of his portraits would never be surpassed.

1 As an illustration for the De Meyer article, Drian made this drawing of Chanel.
2 The engaging Baron Gayne De Meyer.
3 Illustration of a dress by Chanel in *Vogue*, 1924. The waistline falls below the hips.

MLLE CHANEL TELLS BARON DE MEYER HER OPINIONS ON GOOD TASTE

This headline, which ran in a 1923 issue of *Harper's Bazaar*, marked a turning point in Chanel's career, for the recognition of Baron De

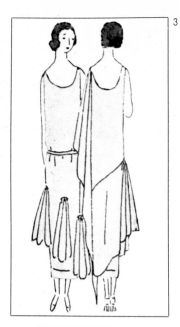

1920–24: the Chanel style turns its back on the past

1920–24 was the period when Chanel became an international figure. She was sought after and invited everywhere, which constituted a significant departure in the annals of society, for "1900 did not receive its *fournisseurs*, even if they were Monsieur Doucet and Madame Lanvin," as Morand correctly noted in his book on Chanel. About this brief period in society, Chanel could say with pride: "I did not go into society because I had to design clothes. I designed clothes precisely because I did go into society, because I was the first to live the life of this century." Still speaking to Morand, she gave this apt definition of fashion—*la mode:* "Fashion is not simply a matter of clothes; fashion is in the air, borne upon the wind; one intuits it; it is in the sky and on the macadam; it comes from ideas, manners, events. . . . If, for example, there

are no more *robes d'intérieur*—those tea gowns so dear to the heroines of Bourget and Bataille—it is undoubtedly because we live in an age when there aren't any more interiors." And indeed it was not only fashions that changed in these years. Textiles, colors, architecture, furniture—everything was in the process of changing. It was all moving toward the explosion of 1925, for the world itself was undergoing change. But had one told Gabrielle that she was hitting her stride at a historic moment, would she have understood? Whole pieces of the past were simply crumbling away. How could Chanel have known, she who, as it happened, had no past? This was her tremendous advantage. No woman could have been less concerned about her social success. "Society" had never before opened its doors to *couturières*, however tal-

ented they may have been, and these creative women had been relegated to the status of *faiseuses* or "dressmakers" (with the word *couturier* used only in the masculine). Then, suddenly, for Chanel everything changed. But it all seemed perfectly natural to her, as natural as the revolution in style that she helped to bring about.

4 The creations of *haute couture* were shamelessly copied. Only Chanel said that the practice seemed inevitable, making it better to pay no heed. Here at the races in 1922, a lineup of fake Chanels.
5 Misia in Venice in 1921, the year she met Chanel, a talented beauty until then hardly known to her. But Misia sensed that Chanel would cut a brilliant figure in festive Paris and thus introduced the designer into

above Misia in Venice in 1921, the year of her first encounter with Chanel, a gifted beauty whom she had scarcely heard of. Sensing that Chanel would cut a brilliant figure in festive Paris, Misia introduced the *couturière* to her friends in the Ballets Russes, the exclusive realm over which she reigned.
right Misia in a chair borne by Diaghilev, Sert, Lifar. Pompeii, 1925.

the exclusive realm over which she reigned—the social and artistic circle centering upon the Ballets Russes.

6 Diaghilev, José-Maria Sert, and Sergei Lifar all serving as bearers for the chair occupied by Misia Sert. Pompeii, 1925.

7 Drawing published in *Vogue*, 1924. Chanel not only lowered the waistline but vigorously emphasized the drop.

8 On January 21, 1924, Lenin died, and Stalin came to power. This forced the émigrés to see the Revolution as real, not a passing cataclysm but an irreversible situation. And in the salons of Chanel a whole new wave of aristocrats found employment. During the lunch break they met at a little tearoom called Aux Fleurs in the Faubourg Saint-Honoré. Among them was Count Koutousov, now the head recep-

tionist at Chanel's, after having been the governor of the Crimea. His stories astonished, as when he stated that his celebrated ancestor had been completely drunk the day he got the best of Napoleon's troops. Also in the group working at Chanel's was Baron de Retern. He became famous when one day, to lift his depression, he took a taxi and snapped: "To the Baltic!" The startled chauffeur simply asked the general direction, whereupon the imperturbable Baron replied: "Toward the north." Improvising, they had progressed as far as Chantilly when the driver finally persuaded his passenger to give up the journey and return to the Chanel salon.

9 Drawing of a Chanel dress in *Vogue*, 1924. Now young women scandalized their mothers with a new set of gestures, such as applying their lipstick in public.

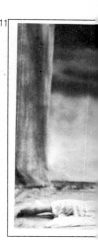

1920–25: emancipated women and innovators

1 *La Garçonne* appeared in July 1922 and quickly became the novel people were snatching out of one another's hands. It created a scandal, causing the author to be stricken from the rolls of the Legion of Honor.

2 Chanel invented beach pajamas, here seen in their first version. A woman in pants! The sight created panic in Garches. Never had anyone seen *that!*

3 Berings, drawing in *L'Illustration*, August, 1925. At La Potinière in Deauville women began to smoke like men.

4 Coiffure *à la garçonne*, which the press derisively termed *au poilu de 2e classe*, a slang reference to the razored recruits of 1914–18. In this ad for Campari the model's neck has been shaved after a manner adopted in Italy.

5 "Into the water! Into the water! The battle cry of 1925," announced *L'Illustration*. Here, little Orlandi, from the "happy band" of Royallieu, still the *irregulière* of Bayon Foy, has improvised a bathing robe.

6 Rather than wearing a bowler hat for the Deauville races, Baron Foy affected a casual look.

7 Berings, drawing in *L'Illustration*, 1925: "Many women in bathing suits have a masculine and somewhat singular appearance. They look like boys who have just taken their *baccalauréat*."

8 At Garches, Henri Bernstein adopted the same pajamas worn by Chanel. Here was the first manifestation of the unisex style.

10–11 Short, short hair or even a man's suit no longer sufficed as a symbol around which the great pioneers of Sapphism could rally. Mathilde de Morny—seen here as Napoleon and in a mime drama with Colette—has been completely surpassed.

12 Stravinsky opted for French citizenship. He left Switzerland in 1920 and, accompanied by his family, moved in with Chanel, remaining there about two years. It was in 1922 that the composer sent this photo to Diaghilev, inscribed: "I send you this questionable copy of a good photo of my mug, a family-type photo." Stravinsky was very smitten with Chanel, who all her life would cherish the icon that he gave her on his arrival in her home, where under commission from Diaghilev he orchestrated the themes for the ballet *Pulcinella*.

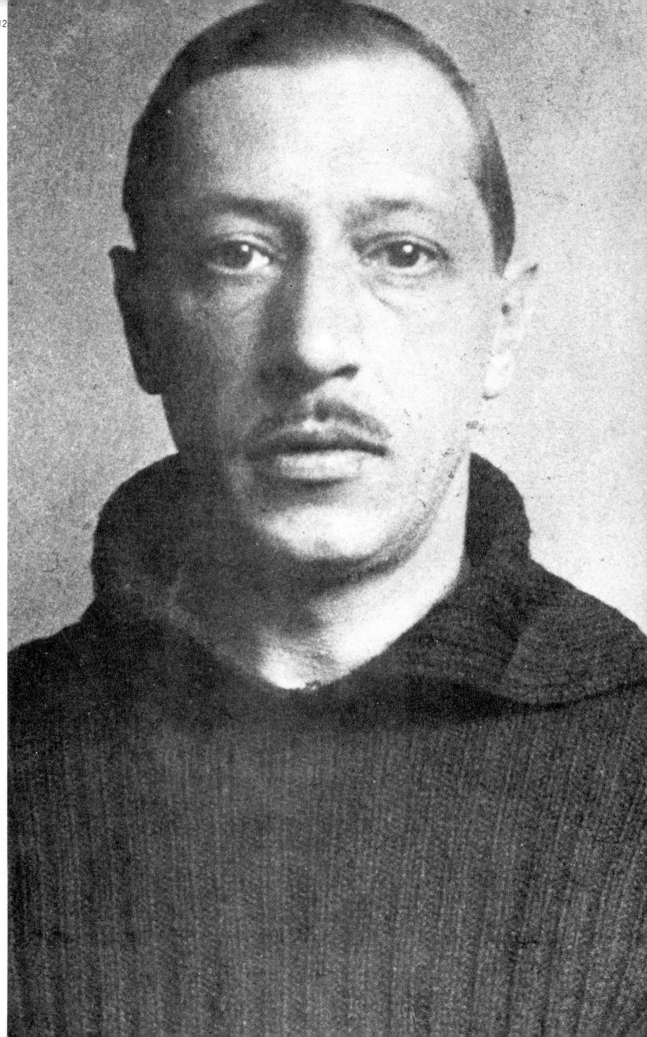

Diaghilev takes the "Blue Train"

In January 1924 Diaghilev found himself so seduced by the music of Christiné and Yvain and the popular forms of French operetta that he began to think of commissioning a scenario in that spirit. Deliver ballet from its mists and veils and give it a touch of reality—who could better effect such a renewal than Jean Cocteau? With *Le Boeuf sur le toit* and then with *Les Mariés de la tour Eiffel,* he had already shown the way. Thus, it was to Cocteau that Diaghilev took his idea. *Le Train bleu,* a ballet combining acrobatics, satire, and pantomime, came forth as a "danced operetta."

1 Sergei de Diaghilev, whom Igor Markevitch characterized as a "prodigious *agent provocateur*," had this very quality in common with Jean Cocteau. For his "Blue Train" music, Diaghilev went to Darius Milhaud, who found the request most unusual: "I had never thought of writing an operetta . . . even without words. I accepted the challenge." The two collaborators are shown here.
2 For the choreography, Diaghilev wanted Bronislava Nijinska, seen here seated with the great impresario and Boris Kochno, who was Diaghilev's personal secretary and artistic advisor to the Ballets Russes.

a program illustrated by Picasso

Beginning in 1923, Boris Kochno became responsible for the creation of the program for the Ballets Russes performances. In this capacity, he made a vain attempt to get Picasso's permission to reproduce the studies of the company dancers that the painter had made in Rome in 1917. Unfortunately, the sketches could not be found in the indescribable disorder of Picasso's studio. Then, just as Kochno was about to give up, "Picasso, as if seized by a sudden inspiration," said the Russian, "took a pencil from his pocket and, in a matter of minutes, covered the maquette, page by page, with the most wonderful drawings." Reproduced here, these drawings appeared in the *Train bleu* program, making it a sumptuous publication indeed.

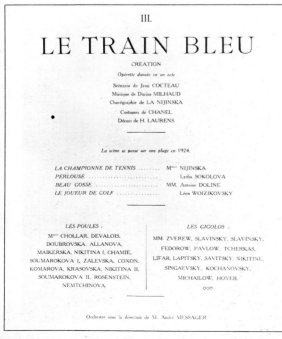

144

choreography inspired by sport

The "Blue Train"—France's famous Paris-Riviera express—had already left when the curtain went up on the ballet bearing this title. And it would never appear. But the very term sufficed to evoke a certain period luxury, with its René Prou marquetry and Lalique accessories. Instead of the Blue Train, it was the passengers that the ballet put on stage, there giving themselves up to the pleasures of the beach. Among them *Beau Gosse* ("Handsome Boy") and Perlouse. Some were odd in both *métier* and name, such as the Gigolos and the *Poules* (meaning "hens" but also prostitutes and the third person in a quadrille); others were sports stars: the Golfer and the Tennis Champion. What Jean Cocteau wanted to re-create was a synthesis of modern life in all its newness.

Premiered in June 1924 at the Théâtre des Champs-Elysées, *Le Train bleu* formed part of "the season of art at the 8th Olympiad," in which Diaghilev's Ballets Russes proved to be the main event. Baron de Coubertin, president of the Olympic Committee, and the members of the Committee, all present and cited, filled the hall and two pages of the program.

As Armand Lanoux has noted in his study of the years around 1925: "The only revolution, basically, is sport. 1900 had the velocipede, horses, the first racing cars; 1925 brought athleticism, boxing, the stadium. . . ." To give choreographic expression to a scenario bringing together bathers, tennis players, golf champions, and beautiful young things in search of adventure, Diaghilev chose Bronislava Nijinska, who was as stubborn as her illustrious brother. She spoke not a word of French and, moreover, knew nothing about the famous Blue Train to the south of France. Separated from the Ballets Russes throughout the war, detained in Russia, and deeply marked by the Revolution, she had no taste for either luxury or laughter. Cocteau suggested that she seek inspiration in photographs of Suzanne Lenglen playing tennis and of the Prince of Wales on the golf course. Both failed to move her. Diaghilev himself served as interpreter and mediator, but right away Cocteau and Nijinska began to detest each other. She reserved for herself the role of the Tennis Player. Small and heavily muscled, she was, like Nijinsky, rather short of leg, and with her fleshy mouth and almond eyes, she very much resembled her brother. She also had his strength and talent. Diaghilev thought her the great choreographer of her time: "Whatever one may think, that extravagant little lady . . . comes from the Nijinsky family, which says everything."

1 Opening night for *Le Train bleu*. From left to right: Perlouse, danced by Sokolova (Hilda Munnings from England and, in 1913, the first non-Russian *première* ever engaged by Diaghilev); Beau Gosse, in the person of Dolin;

Cocteau, the scenarist; Golf Player, a role taken by Leon Woizikovski, brought from Poland in 1915; and the Tennis Player, the part that Nijinska reserved for herself.
2 Suzanne Lenglen, who at age fifteen was tennis champion of France and who delighted the British with her sensational leaps, served as the model for Cocteau's Tennis Player in *Le Train bleu*. In 1924 the Davis Cup, which was as old as the century, guaranteed an international audience for tennis. But the tennis vogue in France was due mainly to Lenglen, the invincible queen of Wimbledon in singles as well as doubles from 1919 to 1924, the year that she turned professional.
3 Anton Dolin in his gym suit.
4 The way Lenglen had of dressing contributed to her legend. No woman champion before her had ever worn two cardigans, one on top of the other, nor a strip of fabric wound about the head like a bandage. Chanel used this in the headdress she designed for Nijinska.
5 Dolin's acrobatic variation provided one of the great moments of the opening night. It received the greatest applause, by far.

sets by a sculptor: Laurens

It was not a painter but a sculptor who did the set for *Le Train bleu*. A Cubist, Henri Laurens had never in his life prepared a stage design. But it was this most Parisian of Parisians that Diaghilev asked to re-create a fashionable beach scene, this son of a laborer who took on the task of transposing to the theatre the frivolity of a summer holiday. Laurens, like Milhaud, liked a challenge. And he handled the Côte d'Azur *cabines* in a strange way, making them look stripped and truncated. When finished, the set resembled a collage. It completely changed the sense the audience had of the elegant beaches where each day the Blue Train discharged its cargo of bathers. Because of his aesthetic rigor, Laurens—the taciturn artist whose friends were Braque, Gris, Picasso, and Modigliani (the author of a magnificent portrait of a bearded and long-haired Laurens)—had remained unknown to the world of evening galas. The exceptions in this crowd, however, were two famous collectors who happened to be at the *Train bleu* premiere: Jacques Doucet and Charles de Noailles (the one owned a "fountain" and the other a "fireplace" by Laurens). The artist had also been known to Radiguet, whose *Pélicans* he had just finished illustrating. Fame arrived late for Laurens. Only after World War II did he receive the attention he merited. Ironically the proud sculptor had long said: "We are all the products of our time and social environment—that is, if we are not plagiarists of the past."

Picasso's stage curtain

In the spring of 1924 Diaghilev visited Picasso and found himself stopped in his tracks by a painting of two tunic-clad women whose shoulder straps have fallen away to reveal the figures' breasts. As they race along the beach, the women seem ecstatic with sand, sea, and wind—the very image of joyous running. Right off, Diaghilev wanted to make the painting into the forecurtain for *Le Train bleu.* Picasso felt uncertain about the idea, but no one could resist Diaghilev, and so, while unenthusiastic, the artist gave in.

Diaghilev assigned the execution of the curtain to one of his closest collaborators, Prince Schervachidzé, whose talent in such matters bordered on the prodigious. When opening night came and Picasso saw the curtain for the first time, he was so impressed with the work of the Prince-artisan that immediately, at the bottom of a work he had never touched, the master wrote: "Dedicated to Diaghilev." After which, without the slightest hesitation, he signed: "Picasso. 24."

1   The forecurtain for *Le Train bleu,* executed by Prince A. Schervachidzé, after a painting by Picasso. As a salute to the picture, Diaghilev commissioned Georges Auric to compose a fanfare.

costumes bearing the Chanel signature

For the *Train bleu* costumes, Diaghilev went to Chanel, who worked to the very letter of the assignment as given by Cocteau: "Instead of trying to remain this side of the ridiculous in life, to come to terms with it, I would push beyond. What am I looking for? To be truer than true." Thus, *Le Train bleu* was not danced in costumes that mixed the real with the imaginary but in actual sports clothes, which included beach sandals and golf shoes. Chanel made no attempt to prettify but instead adorned the dancers with the charm of reality.

1 The "Beautiful Bather," a costume worn by Lydia Sokolova. Victoria & Albert Museum.
2 Dolin as *Beau Gosse* and Leon Woizikovski in the role of the Golfer.
3 Chanel during the rehearsals for *Le Train bleu*. She brought to the stage a style that was her own.
4 Wearing her swimsuit, Lydia Sokolova in the role of Perlouse, with Leon Woizikovski.

la vogue nègre

It burst upon the scene in 1925, transforming all aspects of daily life. Decorators and ceramists, jewelers and cabinetmakers, silversmiths and bookbinders, silk weavers, poster makers, and glassblowers all "went Negro." Even the Siegel mannequins created by Vigneau for department-store windows were lacquered black. They had what may have been the desired effect, which was to provoke indignant protest.

Negro art had been known since 1905, but only to a very small number of artists and collectors. Suddenly in 1925 it caught the interest of the popular press, thanks mainly to a pair of great successes. First came American jazz, with all its freshness and originality. This brought socialites to the *bals nègres* where they danced the Black Bottom. Fierce competition developed among the *boîtes*—mainly the Balle Nègre and the Boulle Noire—where Parisians could dance with Blacks. All this helped to prepare for the triumph of the *Revue nègre,* which introduced Josephine Baker and Sydney Bechet in secondary roles. With its explosive force, the *Revue nègre* repeated the adventure of the Ballets Russes, revealing to the Paris of 1926 an exotic art of bewitching authenticity.

1 When Josephine Baker made her Paris debut in the chorus of *La Revue nègre,* she was only nineteen and completely unknown. Born in St. Louis, she had sung since the age of eight in the nightclubs of Harlem. In Paris she appeared on stage in the nude and created a sensation. Her beautiful black-idol body, her ravishingly lovely bust, her delicate arms and long legs combined with her agility and exotically charming voice to assure the American performer an instantaneous success. Nothing in the history of French theatre could compare with it. Whereas the Ballets Russes drew an elite class, the *Revue nègre* had immense popular appeal, and it made a star of Josephine overnight. She posed in the nude for Dunand, who made several portraits of her in lacquer and eggshell. Man Ray photographed her, and Horst left this image of the new "rage of Paris." For awhile Josephine made her mark in fashion, encouraging the taste for suntan and shaved armpits. In the words of Pierre Mac Orlan: "Baker, even more than *la Miss* [Mistinguett], shatters our way of seeing and evokes a primitive order."

This was the *order* that Chanel, more than anyone else in Paris, understood how to capture and exploit. She too was thirsting for authenticity and naturalness. Beginning in 1925, the Chanel style would develop and stand for the whole notion of modernity.

2 Drawing in the French edition of *Vogue.* In April 1926 the Chanel collection was worn by models whose coiffure strangely recalled that of Josephine Baker.

AMERIQUE AFRIQUE

MAGIE
NOIRE

PAUL MORAND

The legend of Paul Morand, like that of Chanel, is integral to the midtwenties. The style and tone of Chanel, her art of living all find their echo in Morand's style, tone, and writing. These two lived in harmony with their time, Chanel by dressing it and Morand by describing Europe between the wars, already submerged in a mad wave of jazz.

1 *Magie noire* ("Black Magic") tells of the irresistible and disquieting attraction that the civilized world felt for the Black world, a phenomenon that Morand believed to have begun in 1920: "In the bars of the post-Armistice period, jazz produced such sublime and heart-breaking accents that we all understood that we must have a new form of expressing our own feelings. Sooner or later, I said to myself, we must respond to this call from the dark, must go and see what was behind that imperious melancholy coming out of the saxophones."
2 Here is one of the monarchs of the twenties, dressed in a diving suit. Morand was the biggest sportsman among the writers of his time. Nothing could stop him, and he traveled constantly, from New York to Timbuktu. His philosophy: "The real snobs are in sweaters." Here he simultaneously gave the best definition of the twenties' reverse snobbism and the briefest possible explanation for the success of his friend Chanel. He cultivated a black humor: "After *Black Magic*, even photos of me began—oh Dorian Gray!—to look negroid."

1926:
a veritable frenzy
of black

1   In 1926 the American edition of *Vogue* predicted that a certain black dress created by Chanel—a simple sheath in crêpe-de-chine, with long, closely fitting sleeves—would become a sort of uniform for all women of taste. But hordes of women wearing the same dress? Such a forecast seemed totally irrational. Then, to show its readers that this immense success might be due to the *impersonal* simplicity of the dress, the magazine risked a comparison: Would one hesitate to buy an automobile because it could not be distinguished from another vehicle of the same brand? On the contrary, for the similarity constituted a guarantee of quality. *Vogue* concluded: "Here is a Ford signed 'Chanel.'" At right is the drawing of Chanel's dress published in Paris in 1926.

Despite virulent criticism, Chanel's "Ford" had the reception anticipated for it. It was in vain that male journalists deplored so many suppressions—"no more bosom, no more stomach, no more rump. As for the skirt, we are raising it to the knees"—and they could only resort to irony: "Feminine fashion of this moment in the 20th century will be baptized 'lop off everything.'" It signaled that no longer could men dictate how women should dress. It was with the simplifying taste of Chanel that the female sex would identify.

Thus, fashion too entered the age of standardization, an evolution that has proved irreversible.

1927

The Art Déco style (so-called for the sleek modernism that prevailed at the great 1925 exhibition sponsored in Paris by the Union Central des Arts Décoratifs) proved to be indisputably successful. Never had a call to order been regarded as more imperative. With the new sense of interior décor—stripped of sculpture and all other ornament—fashion would naturally make an alliance, as it did in the Élégance pavilion at the 1925 Expo. Here are two Chanel dresses, one in voile (right) and the other in black satin (below), as they appeared in the Paris *Vogue* of January 1927. These were the dresses that inspired Paul Poiret to utter his famous sortie: "What has Chanel invented? Poverty de luxe." He went on: "Formerly women were architectural, like the prows of ships, and very beautiful. Now they resemble little undernourished telegraph clerks."

pages 158–159 More black, more Chanel, more drawings by Douglas Polland for *Vogue*, and two novelties that generated great excitement: Moroccan crepe and cloche hats, which provoked further irony from the arbiters of past styles: "As for the hats, they are nothing but plain tea strainers in soft felt, into which women plunge their heads by pulling down, with both hands clutching the bottom. . . . Everything disappears, swallowed up by that elastic pocket—hair, forehead, ears, cheeks, all but the nose. They would surely use shoehorns, had this been suggested." Thus spoke Sem.

159

the salon of mirrors

In 1928, on the wave of a prodigious success, Chanel installed her business on three floors at 31 Rue Cambon, where the house would remain for the rest of the founder's life. Within the infinity produced by the reflecting mirrors, total sobriety reigned. This was the vast salon on the *premier étage* where the *haute couture* collections would be presented. A room conceived and constructed to look as if it had no walls, it created an impression of endless space by virtue of its mirror revetments. Simple basin-like chandeliers gave off a concentrated light, which the mirrors multiplied. Altogether, Chanel's grand salon is of real aesthetic significance, for it typifies the transition from the "roaring twenties" to the 1930s.

Business in general sought a décor uniquely suited to its functions, a décor as removed as possible from the pastiches and fake luxury that had prevailed before Expo 25. Chanel was not the only one who opted for a *style moderne*, an interior conforming to the exigencies of her *métier*, but she was certainly the only woman who understood how to invest her professional environment with the maximum of purity and unity.

purloined tweeds

The Duke of Westminster required that his valet iron his shoelaces, even though His Grace cared little that his soles may have been worn through. He cultivated a style of life that Chanel found immensely instructive. "Elegant; that is, detached," she said, as if reviving the philosophy of Reverdy.

1 Bend'or as country gentleman.
2 Chanel while salmon fishing in 1928. Here two friends have confiscated the clothing of their host. Gabrielle and Vera Bate, an English woman, wear his jackets, his sweaters, his pants, and even his shoes. While making for a good laugh, the disguise also served to introduce Chanel to Scotch tweeds.

Vera had been Gabrielle's good angel, for it was she who introduced the *couturière* to Westminster, and she who helped Chanel find her way into English society. "Vera" was simply a name adopted by Sarah Arkwright when she went to work for Chanel in 1925. Despite a birth certificate that declared her to be the daughter of a mason, Vera Bate's relationship to the British royal family cannot be doubted.

in the Prince of Wales set

After having introduced Chanel to Westminster, Vera Bate also presented her to the heir to the English throne.

One day a young man whom the butler had never seen before rang the bell at 29 Faubourg Saint-Honoré. Was this the home of Mademoiselle Chanel? He had an appointment with Vera, he said. Vera was out, but the young man made a fine impression upon the butler. He seemed very proper indeed. After he had spent two hours in the kitchen, carrying on an animated conversation with the chef, Vera finally arrived. When the butler asked whom he should announce, the visitor answered: "The Prince of Wales."

1 Summer 1925, on board the battleship *Repulse*. Edward, Prince of Wales, returning to England at the end of one of his interminable tours, trips that filled him with an increasingly evident boredom. Forty-five different countries received him with acclaim, as much in Africa as in Latin America. But despite the fact that he was still "Prince Charming," the idol of the masses, the first criticisms of him were beginning to appear in the British press, causing concern to the King. Among His Majesty's complaints were the Prince's showy suits, his dreadful horsemanship (photo 3), his spectacular falls, his suede shoes, which to the well-bred were doubly offensive by reason of their evident connotations of homosexuality—indeed everything that

suggested a tendency for the Prince to compromise his future. Published in *L'Illustration* under the title "princely games," the photo above shows Edward *en travesti* for a review given by the ship's officers.
2 The Chanel style in 1927, as seen by *Vogue.* Chanel took a curious kind of revenge. Her models were always seen in the most select settings. Indeed, her dresses seemed designed for the very paddocks from which the beautiful friend of Balsan had for so long been excluded.
3 The Prince of Wales steeplechasing. The King would eventually order him to give up his favorite sport.
4 Chanel on La Bella. Lombardi, a celebrated Italian cavalry officer, kept her horses in form.

Chanel in her English period

From 1926 to 1931 Chanel adopted an English style. She took advantage of everything that charmed her, whether at Eaton Hall or on the Duke of Westminster's yachts, and made these discoveries the dominant themes of her collections. In 1928 the removable waistcoat was born out of the black-sleeved waistcoat, its front striped with the ducal colors, that the valets of Eaton Hall wore for their morning chores. The beret now donned by elegant women, pulled down flush with the eyelids, was that of the sailors on the Westminster yacht, the *Cutty Sark*. But Chanel surprised her friends in London by accompanying her daytime outfits with jewelry of a sort that no lady of English society would have dared to wear except with a ballgown: pearls cascading over the livery waistcoat and on the beret a great cluster of stones. A breeze of sumptuosity was wafting over the creations of Chanel. But it was a highly controlled richness. Never—at any time in her life—did Gabrielle Chanel imagine that luxury could have any purpose other than to make simplicity appear remarkable.

1 The Duke of Westminster on board the *Cutty Sark*, his second yacht, an 83-ton destroyer.
2 Chanel (right) and Marcelle Meyer, the official pianist of Les Six and the Dada soirées, on the *Flying Cloud*, a 4-masted schooner.
3 On the *Flying Cloud*. Hardly on board, His Grace grew impatient for heavy weather. This was what made him happy, for the sea was his passion.
4 Gabrielle Chanel in her English period. On her wrists she wears the bracelets just created for her house by her most recent discovery: Fulco di Verdura. Then just beginning, the Sicilian Duke would make a career in Paris, London, and New York.

sweaters
for *Orpheus*

ties
for the Muses

In 1926 the event of the Paris theatre season was Copeau's surrender of the Théâtre des Arts to Georges and Ludmilla Pitoëff, who forthwith announced a new production: *Orpheus*, a one-act tragedy by Cocteau. This brought Chanel, as *Antigone* had, back to the sources of the Greek tragic spirit, for she was to design the costumes. Now the journey would carry her, in the wake of Orpheus, into the kingdom of the dead. Jean Hugo took charge of the sets and made them resolutely contemporary. Pitoëff himself became the director. From Switzerland, Rilke telegraphed his encouragement: "May Jean [Cocteau] feel the warmth of my admiration, he whose poetry alone penetrates into myth, whence he returns tanned as if he had been on the seashore." The production caused a great critical stir, provoking praise and abuse in equal measure.

1 Ludmilla Pitoëff as Eurydice. Dress by Chanel.
2 Pitoëff as Eurydice with her sweater-clad Orpheus; behind them, Marcel Herran, who played Heurtebise, a role that Cocteau himself would assume in 1927.

In 1929 Chanel rediscovered her admirer from the days in Garches, Stravinsky, who for awhile had made his home in the *couturière's* villa after his return from Switzerland. During the intervening years Stravinsky had ceased to work with the ballet. The last time he composed for it was in 1920. Now *Apollon musagète* would revive his fruitful collaboration with Diaghilev. Written for strings, this ballet marked Stravinsky's return to classicism. It also joined the artist's name to that of a compatriot whose choreographic inventions were already astounding balletomanes. This was a young Georgian named Balanchivadzé, which Diaghilev abbreviated to Balanchine. Sets and costumes had been assigned to Bauchant, who, however, refused to cooperate with anyone. Without a mock-up of the costumes, Diaghilev improvised, with results that, while satisfactory for Apollo, proved disastrous for the Muses. Called to the rescue, Chanel visualized a free adaptation of the antique tunic, whose pleats she bound with tie silk.

3 Dressed by Chanel, Felia Doubrovska as a Muse in *Apollon musagète*.

3

death in Venice

The voyage made by the *Flying Cloud* in 1929 was a strange one. It included the brusque and continuous presence of Misia, at a time when Bend'or and Gabrielle were about to break up. But Misia had good reason to get away from Paris, where Sert was making her suffer his new and all-too-evident passion, Roussy Mdivani, a Georgian princess obsessed with a longing for self-destruction. An ongoing source of amusement for Parisian society in these years was the spectacle provided by the Sert-Mdivani triangle.

Docking in Venice, Misia and Gabrielle went off in search of Diaghilev. A telegram had alerted Misia that the great impresario was on the Lido, very ill and poorly cared for. His diabetic condition had rapidly deteriorated. Misia and Gabrielle reached him on August 17, 1929, in his room, where, although bedridden, he played the cheerful charmer. But a calm of finality seemed to have come over him. Misia left convinced that he was lost. That evening Diaghilev told Boris Kochno of the pleasure the visit from such loyal friends had given him. He kept repeating: "They were so young, all in white! They were so white."

By the night of August 18–19 Diaghilev was dying. Misia ran to his bedside, and was there when in the early morning he breathed his last.

As usual, the treasury of the Ballet Russes was empty and actually burdened with a huge deficit. It could not even afford to give Sergei de Diaghilev a decent funeral. Chanel stepped in and paid all expenses.

In the gray hour of early dawn, a gondola bore the body of this prodigious man to San Michele, Venice's "Island of the Dead." The escort consisted of five friends: Kochno, Lifar, Misia, Catherine d'Erlanger, and Gabrielle Chanel. At the latter's suggestion, the three women took Diaghilev's last words as the expression of a wish. Thus, seated in the black gondola, they were dressed "all in white."

1 Chanel, whose reputation in Italy was growing, abandoned Deauville for Venice. Here, on the Lido beach, Gabrielle and Misia, two friends "all in white," with Madame Philippe Berthelot in black.
2 In 1929 on the Lido, Gabrielle Chanel launched the first beach pajamas, leaving to her competitors the responsibility for shorts, which she vehemently resisted as an absurd style. Here, a consolidated trio uniformly wearing pajamas: Countess Étienne de Beaumont (wife of the famous Parisian Maecenas and a Chanel client), Gabrielle, and Misia Sert. The two ladies in shorts—Countess Moretti and Madame Chiesa—were the leading hostesses of Venice's *beaux soirs*.
3 The funeral mask of Sergei de Diaghilev.

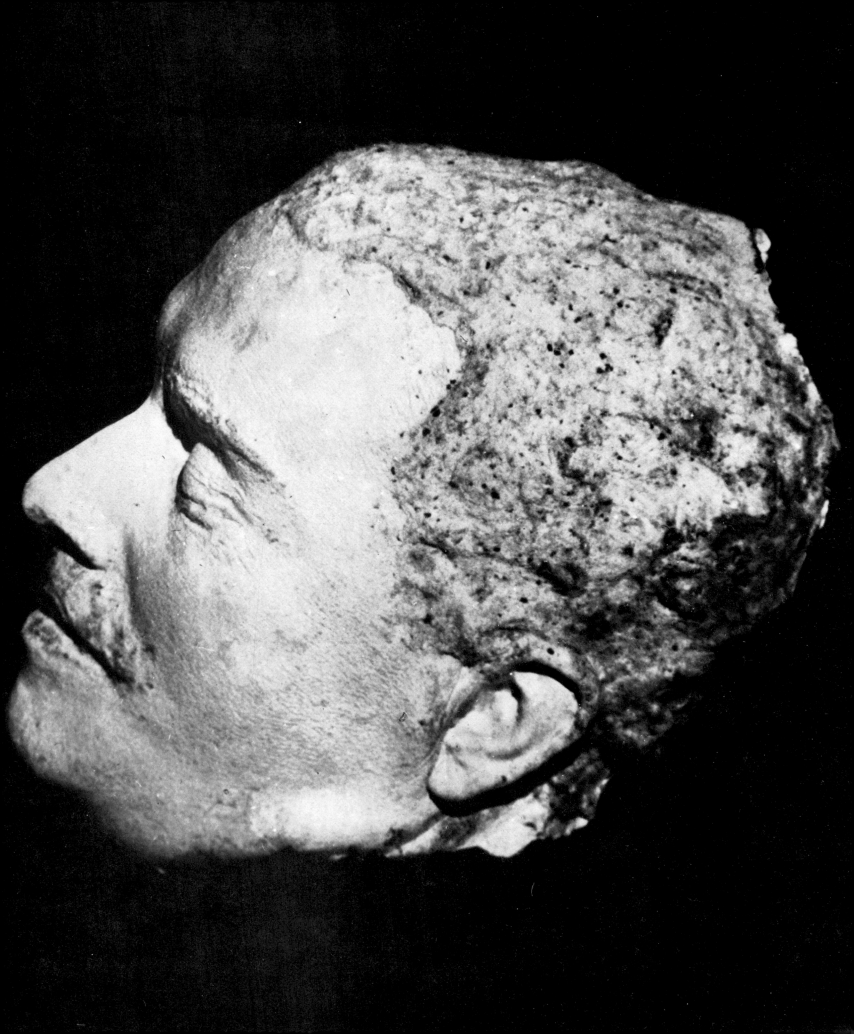

Cocteau/Chanel,
a creative friendship

1932–37 were years in which Chanel's life was
much affected by her lively friendship with
Cocteau and, on the creative level, by her own
growing powers of invention. By now, the *couturière's* reputation had attained world-wide
proportions. And these years, which were so
important for Chanel, had their echo in the
work of Cocteau, who now developed a passion
for drawing and an interest in journalism. In
1932 he did the portrait of his collaborator reproduced below, and throughout the period
he also produced many drawings of her dress
designs, all commissioned for publication in
the most prestigious foreign journals. Jean
Cocteau, whose friendship could never be
accused of self-interest, continued to seek
Chanel's involvement in his theatrical under-
takings. In 1934 the poet rediscovered the
myth of the Holy Grail and transformed it into
a new play for the Théâtre de l'Oeuvre. Presented in 1937, *The Knights of the Round Table*
was played in costumes designed by Gabrielle
Chanel.

1   Jean Cocteau in 1935 at the time of his *Por-
traits-Souvenirs* for *Le Figaro*.
2   A Chanel design as drawn by Cocteau.
3   Chanel portrayed by Cocteau, 1932.

Egypt according to Paul Iribe and Cecil B. De Mille

Iribe's power in Hollywood, unlike De Mille's, was not so great that he could be utterly odious without affecting the loyalty and commitment of his team. De Mille was worshipped in the California studios, whereas Iribe made few friends there. Were they all trying to make him pay for his stormy rise? Certainly, Iribe's relations with Mitchell Leisen, one of the best costume designers in Hollywood and, moreover, a faithful member of De Mille's staff, quickly deteriorated into open hostility, plunging the two men into one of the cinema's guerrilla wars, often erupting into strong words, shouting, quarrels, fistfights, and always resulting in the dismissal of one or the other of the belligerents. In 1923 it was Leisen who lost the battle, which left Iribe alone to create the costumes and sets for a colossal undertaking: *The Ten Commandments*. Produced and directed by De

Mille, this film brought the Bible to life. It also had an enormous box-office success.

A new promotion in 1924 had Paul Iribe, with De Mille's blessing, improvising as director of *Changing Husbands*. It produced a critical disaster. *The New York Times* went so far as to call the film absurd and its direction actually "amateurish." Only Leatrice Joy was spared.

Right away, De Mille thought it wise to make up with Mitchell Leisen. When the great man put *The King of Kings* into production, he reorganized his staff and restored Leisen as head of the costume department, while leaving the artistic direction to Iribe. Harry Warner would play the leading role: Christ. But a crisis developed in the Golgotha scene, causing De Mille to accuse Iribe of negligence. How was Warner to be held on the Cross? And his hands? How were they going to bleed? None of this had

been prepared. De Mille decided to sacrifice someone and right there. Thus, on the summit of this Golgotha it was not Christ who fell victim but Iribe. Fired! Leisen, on condition that he never again have to work with the Frenchman, agreed to take his place. Iribe left Hollywood without any hope of returning there. But in Paris he was greeted by a present from his American wife: a shop on the Rue du Faubourg Saint-Honoré, its façade gleaming with the new owner's name set forth upon a lacquer ground. This took Iribe back to his true love: the decorative arts.

The photos on this page come from *The Ten Commandments*, produced and directed by Cecil B. De Mille, with costumes and sets by Paul Iribe. The latter's Egypt, beautiful but hardly Biblical, was an Egypt of the twenties, a place of gilt and lacquer.

Iribe and Poiret, decorators

1924: *L'Illustration* inaugurated a series of "visits" to Parisian interiors with a piece on *"le* home *exotique et audacieusement moderne"* of a performing artist: Mademoiselle Spinelly. A tart and peppery singer, she had been formed in the hard school of *café-concert* and, like Maurice Chevalier, had made her debut in the streets of Montmartre, playing before an audience of laborers. Around 1901 she was found to have the talent of a *chanteuse gaie*. By 1922 Spinelly had made the cover of *L'Illustration* in a portrait by J.-G. Domergue. But true consecration came in 1924, when Poiret decorated her "studio" and Iribe her bedroom. This Spinelly, if contemporary accounts are to be believed, was a distinctively Parisian personality: "Perched upon an orange divan, drawing about her a multi-

colored cloak, lamé, embroidered, and trimmed in monkey fur, set before a red-lacquer screen, and flanked by white parrots and a crystal basin, Spinelly is almost *excessively* the woman of today."

4 The neo-Pompeian atrium, with a floor in gold mosaic and a huge skylight supported by lacquered columns. Decorating the walls are reliefs of trees with gilded leaves. At the center, a mirror-lined pool.

Confronted with such an orgy of ideas, one can only repeat Chanel's remark: "Let us beware of originality; in couture it leads to costume, and to theatre in interior design."

5 The bedroom: "It is again Paul Iribe whom Mlle Spinelly asked to design her bedroom: dressing table in rare woods, vast wrought-iron bed upon which a doll reigns among the cushions. Lapis-lazuli columns support, like a ceiling, a huge canopy made of gold-lamé silk. Don't be surprised if, in this setting, you see Spinelly get up wearing the kimono of an Oriental princess or in pajamas by Poiret." *L'Illustration.*

1 The dining room done in the English manner, but a manner reinvented by Paul Iribe. The floor made of white marble set with green strips.
2 A corner of the atrium, created by the atelier of Martine, a concern of considerable fame founded by Paul Poiret in 1912. Note the profusion of cushions on the divan.
3 Domergue, portrait of "Spi." A prominent star, Spinelly was successful in London and the United States as well as in Paris.

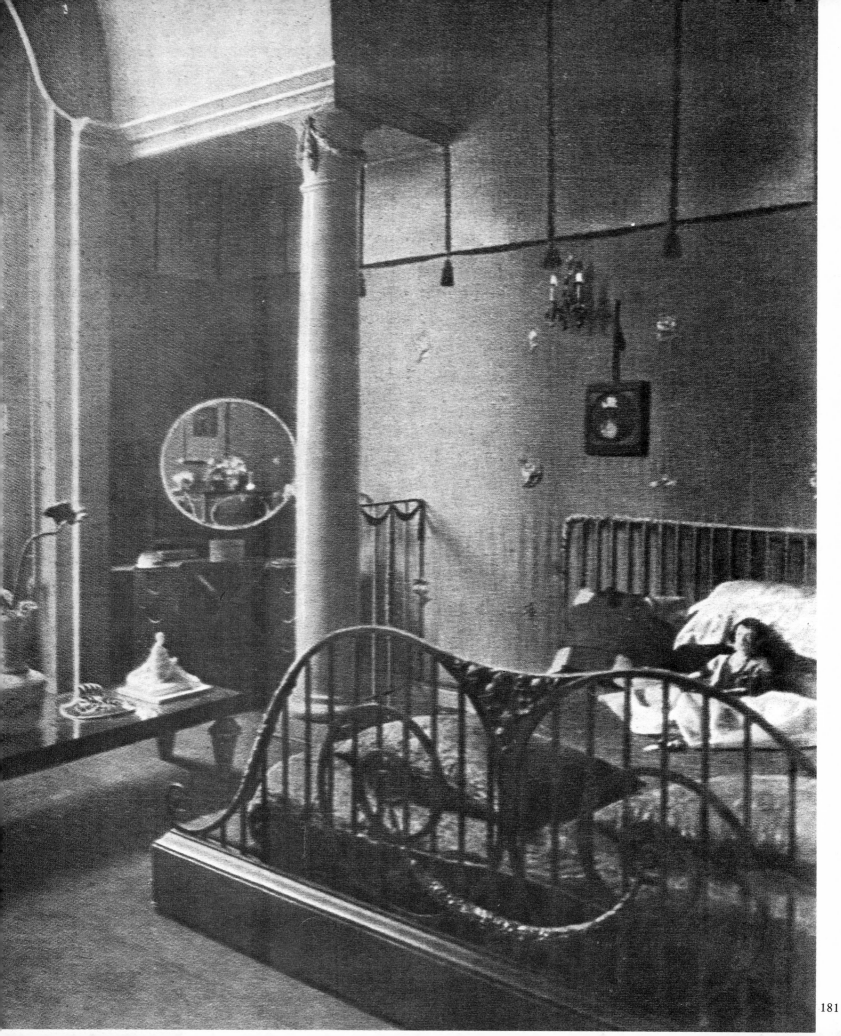

181

a little black bull

Where and when did Colette meet Chanel? Certainly these two knew one another in the twenties, if only through Misia Sert, whose rather close relationship with the great writer is confirmed in the latter's *Journal intermittent*. Between Colette and Chanel, however, feelings were not so friendly. It appears that something other than friendship drew them together—perhaps a sense of revenge upon a past that in some respects was similar for the two women. Before their "success," they both had known not only social opprobrium but also the stern law of necessity. Then too there was their common love of fine craftsmanship, which meant so much to Colette, as can be seen in her portrait of Chanel absorbed in her work, written in 1932 and published in *Prisons et Paradis*.

"If every human face bears a resemblance to some animal—beaked, muzzled, nostriled, trunked, maned—then Mademoiselle Chanel is a small black bull. Is there something of the Camargue here [France's cattle-raising region]? Auvergne asserting its primitive stock. . . . But never mind, for in her butting energy, in her way of facing up to things, of listening, in the defensiveness that sometimes raises a barricade across her face, Chanel is a black bull. That tuft of dark, curly hair, the attribute of bull-calves, falls over her brow all the way to her eyelids and dances with every movement of her head. It is in . . . her work that one must see this reflective conqueror.

"She is said to be very rich. Luckily, she remains uninfected by the contagious glitter of gold, the indiscreet glow exuded by weak souls overwhelmed with possessions.

"There she is, her heels dug into raw materials, between pilasters of jersey, beams of printed foulards, piles of them. Long streams of rolled satin shimmer—a chaos of elastic masonry whose collapse makes no noise whatever. The very walls of the room swell with mute flannels, downy woolens—all here is silence. A figure, silent except for a ready murmur of acquiescence, holds her breath: Mademoiselle Chanel is engaged in sculpting an angel 6 feet tall. A golden-blond angel, impersonal, seraphically beautiful, provided one disregards the rudimentary carving, the paucity of flesh, and the cheerlessness—one of those angels who brought the devil to earth.

"The angel—still incomplete—totters occasionally under the two creative, severe, kneading arms that press against it. Chanel works with ten fingers, nails, the edge of the hand, the palms, with pins and scissors right on the garment, which is a white vapor with long pleats, splashed with crushed crystal. Sometimes she falls to her knees before her work and grasps it, not to worship but to punish it again, to tighten over the angel's long legs—to constrain—some expansion of tulle. . . . Ardent humility, of a body before its preferred work. With her loins taut and her feet tucked under her thighs, Chanel is like a prostrated laundress beating her linens, like those demanding manageresses who train and entreat day after day, twenty times a day, like the quick genuflections of nuns. This professional involvement of the body leaves her thin and hollow with fatigue. At such a moment I see the nape of her neck, which is devoured by black hair, hair that grows with a vegetal vigor. She talks while working, in a low, deliberately contained voice. She talks, teaching and admonishing, with a sort of exasperated patience. I can make out reiterated words, hummed like basic musical motifs: 'I have a horror of *petits machins*. . . . How many times must I say that fullness is slenderizing? I will not allow myself to say it again. . . . Press down there, ease up here. . . . No, *petits machins* are not needed on a fabric that can speak for itself. . . . Bear down here, release it from there on. . . . No, don't skimp. . . . I won't allow myself to repeat. . . .'

"That meekness, which Chanel exacts—and obtains—from herself surprises me more than her authority, because I have read on her face what is most legible: two long, black, unplucked eyebrows, despotic, apt to come together, raise, and lower—above all, lower!—quivering every time they are annoyed by the dancing tuft of hair. . . . From these eyebrows one's attention moves down to the mouth, but there I am not so sure, for in moments of concentration and discontent the middle of the face seems to become concave, sucked in, drawn back under the hood of the eyebrows, under the black volute of hair. It's no more than an instant, but one of total silence, of fierce retreat, a momentary petrification from which the mouth suddenly escapes—the lips flexing, corners turned down, impatient, tamed, punished by cutting teeth. . . .

"The angel-mannequin has left. Another, red-haired seraphim has replaced her, and she too leaves. Then, it is a sort of deity, glistening—to tell the truth—so much so that she seems to have fallen from Heaven, head-first, into a barrel of molasses. . . . As each celestial creature passes Chanel dreams of giving her some earthly attachment, because I hear that low, obstinate voice: 'Take off these *petits machins*. . . . Don't add anything to the *décolleté*. . . . I want to see the wrist, the neck. . . . Here, look at what I am doing. . . .'

"A pause brings back my attention. Mademoiselle Chanel rests standing up like a thoroughbred horse, even eats this way, eating a *petit pain* with bites that send crumbs flying up to the ceiling—as our ancestors used to say.

"Finally, two dark fires dart at me from under the thick tuft, making me think of the gay humor of the little black bull in a time of recreation. . . . But no. Not yet. Putting down her bread-flute, Chanel lovingly handles some antelope leather, soft, worked, polished, melting, with a fur lining that is still more suave. 'It's for me, that, it's for me! Finally, a garment for me! Oh, how good it will feel to be so warm! A good fur-lined garment that is good and light, very snug. . . .' She closes her eyes and, with a distinctively feminine gesture, presses it against her cheek, the sheared fur and its wild odor, and I begin to entone about slow walks in the winter air and napping in the automobile, all under an antelope coat. With my eyes closed, I can suddenly see two pupils the color of spangled granite. The color of mountain water in the crevices of a rock bathed in sunlight—but Mademoiselle Chanel flatly rejects my suggestions of fur-muffled idleness: 'That? It's to go boar hunting in.' "

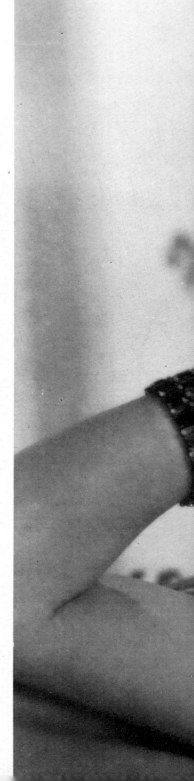

the Chanel-Iribe affair

and Colette's opinion of it

"*Mon chéri*, what a beautiful day! How can I characterize such weather. One would have to do it in music. So much freshness, warmth, sweetness—who could describe all that?" Colette at Saint-Tropez during grape harvest; Colette the Taurian, with her terrace and the cicadas of her garden; Colette with something of a witch about her and dreadfully abrupt when faced with people who pleased her little—all this is expressed in a letter that she wrote in July 1933 to Maurice Goudeket, the man she had lived with for eight years and would marry two years later. A happy period for Colette. At age sixty, she had found a companion worthy of her and in him, according to her friend Marguerite Moréno, "the possibility of a lovely adventure and perhaps more than a lovely adventure." The time was also a happy one for Chanel, who evidently believed that finally, in the person of Paul Iribe, she had met the man of her life. But Colette had her doubts about Iribe, sensing something demonic in him. "As I was making a purchase at Vachon's, a pair of hands clapped over my eyes, a nice body pressing against my back. . . . It was Misia, full of kisses and tender regards. 'Imagine finding you here?' 'Of course, I'm here,' etc. But she had something more urgent for my ear. 'You know, she's marrying him.' 'Who?' 'Iribe. Oh my dear, what an incredible story: Coco's in love for the first time in her life!' Then followed much commentary, etc., etc. 'Oh! I assure you he knows his business, that one.' I didn't have time to ask what business. 'We've been looking for you, even went to your place. We want to take you to dinner in Saint-Raphaël, in Cannes, in . . . .' I decline, kiss, and leave with Moune [the wife of the painter Luc Albert-Moreau]. We then went to pick up Kessel [brother of the writer Joseph Kessel] who was buying something or other. Hardly three steps away a pair of arms throw themselves about me. They belonged to Le Gaseau [the wife of playwright Henri Bernstein] and her daughter. More protestations of love, etc. 'We've been looking for you. I want to take you to Robert de Rothschild's, to Valescure . . . ,' etc. She already knew I had been named drama critic for the *Journal*. More effusions and kisses. We start out again, Moune and I, only to be stopped a few paces along by yet another embrace. . . . It was the Vals [Valentine Fauchier-Magnan]! 'I've just come from your place, looking for you so that I can take you to dinner at L'Escale with . . . ,' etc. I decline, I decline—repeatedly. Moune and I set off for yet another three steps before

my eyes are covered by a new set of hands, this time very fine, cold ones. It was Coco Chanel. Effusions— of a more reserved order. 'I'm taking you to dinner at L'Escale,' etc. I decline once more, and a little farther along I catch sight of Iribe, throwing me kisses. Then, before I can complete the rite of exorcism, he embraces me, tenderly squeezing my hand between his cheek and shoulder. 'How naughty you are, treating me like a demon!' 'And even then you don't give up?' I say. But he went on overflowing with joy and affection. Altogether he's seen sixty years and twenty springtimes. He is slender, lined, and white-haired, and laughs through a set of brand-new teeth. He coos like a dove, which makes it all the more interesting, because you will find in old texts that demons assume the voice and form of the bird of Venus." Why did Colette dread Iribe so much that she began making the gestures of exorcism as he approached?

1 Colette, in a photograph by Henri Lartigue. Then fifty-three, the author had just bought La Treille Muscate ("The Muscat Arbor") in Saint-Tropez, where she would spend the whole of her summers. She had been applauded for what proved to be her last appearance on the stage. This was in *The Vagabond,* an enterprise in which her coproducer had been the totally bankrupt Poiret. *La Revue de Paris* compared Colette to "a Renoir with luscious arms." But Goudeket, at their first encounter, found her *trop en chair* ("too plump"), which in no way prevented his being immediately captivated. Gabrielle Chanel, who had great admiration for Colette, nevertheless took a severe attitude toward the great writer's stoutness: "She positively swaggers in gluttony. The whole of Saint-Tropez is astonished."
2 Paul Iribe photographed in 1933.
3 *Vendeuses*, mannequins . . . the whole Chanel team celebrating *la Sainte-Catherine.* Gabrielle and Iribe in the back row on the left.

Misia alone

She was over fifty and no longer the lush young woman who had turned the heads of Bonnard, Vuillard, and Renoir. She had changed; she had suffered. Now it was Gabrielle Chanel who sustained this friend in a trying time just as she had been supported by Misia at an earlier moment. From 1927 through 1929, while Misia agonized through the collapse of her relationship with José-Maria Sert, Chanel took her away from Paris. The two friends could be seen in England and then in Italy. At home, Misia struggled to accommodate the passion her husband had for the young Georgian, Roussy Mdivani. For a while their *ménage à trois* created almost as much astonishment as the famous Colette-Willy-Polaire triangle. In *Venises*, Morand wrote in 1928 of an encounter at the Villa Malcontenta with "Sert, flopped into a sagging armchair and flanked by his two wives stretched out at his feet." But Misia resisted neither a divorce from Sert nor his remarriage. Unhappy but free, she remained as much the queen of the artistic world as ever, still gathering about her the legendary masters whose genius she had inspired.

When Reverdy sought exile at the abbey of Solesmes, it was Misia who enabled him to succeed. When Marcelle Meyer, who had made the music of Les Six known to the world, found herself passing through a difficult period, Misia revived her in 1933, by renting the great hall at the Hôtel Continental and arranging a two-piano concert. While Poulenc turned the pages, the audience followed a program embellished with a quatrain by Max Jacob, who had entitled the poem: A MÍTIA AMICITIA.

1 Drawing published in 1927 with this legend: "When receiving for dinner, Mme J.-M. Sert, in a georgette creation by Chanel, wears her magnificent triple-length chain of diamonds. Also by Chanel, the simple red jersey." Mentioned in the same caption was the red overcoat worn by Madame Gentien's Arabian gazelle-hound, dressed, like its mistress, by Chanel.
2 Misia, gowned by Chanel for a *fête*, the "Balloon Ball" given in Sert's studio. She learned to adapt to the period's style without sacrificing what had characterized her throughout the years: a sumptuous Slavitude.

Chanel in Hollywood

In 1929 a memorable encounter took place. The setting was Monaco and the intermediary, Dmitri of Russia. This descendant of the Tsars arranged an introduction between Chanel and Sam Goldwyn, the tsar of Hollywood. Faced with the unprecedented crisis then gripping the United States, Goldwyn wanted to give women renewed reason to go to the movies. In the course of an interview, he disclosed his plan. Women would attend the cinema: "*Primo* for the films and the stars, *secondo* to see the

Hollywood. The contract he drew up was to guarantee her a fabulous sum of money: $1 million. This was because the movie mogul wanted the French *couturière* not only to costume the queens of Hollywood but also to reform their taste. It was a ukase: the gorgeous creatures had henceforth to be dressed exclusively by Chanel in their private lives as well as on the screen. But could the stars be counted on to submit?

After long negotiations, Chanel acceded to Goldwyn's wishes and agreed to go to California. Her first visit occurred in April 1931, with Misia Sert going along for the trip. Chanel, however, could not endure being subordinated to stars who refused to have a style imposed upon them, even the Chanel style. With this outcome, Sam Goldwyn was left holding the bag.

1 Chanel in 1931. From Garbo to Stroheim, from Dietrich to Cukor, everyone felt honored to be involved with her, a woman the local press described as "the greatest mind that fashion has ever known."
2 Wearing the same suit as Chanel, Gloria Swanson in *Tonight or Never*, a movie that premiered in December 1931.

a certain notion of luxury

In 1928 Chanel went to the heights of Roque-brunne and made herself a present of an olive grove and a view of extraordinary beauty overlooking the Mediterranean. A royal acquisition, it consisted of a summer house—her first vacation home. Chanel was then forty-five years old. Finished in less than a year, the house—architecture and decoration alike—re-

flected its creator's habitual rigor. The style of La Pausa would virtually found a school.

Here Chanel sought the natural above all else, thereby affirming her aversion to fussy and facile effects. It was a house in which to live the life of the times. On the interior, it displayed whitewashed walls and few objects. In the garden, under the century-old olive trees, reigned a single color—the blue of lavender. While her friends sensed an air of the convent, Chanel declared that she had advised her architect to visit a monastery where, as a child, "she has spent marvelous vacations." In truth, she had sent him to Aubazine, to that orphanage whose severe beauty continued, secretly, to haunt her.

above   Gabrielle Chanel at La Pausa.

190

how to use
the *beau monde*

Confidences from Chanel reported by Morand: "I have used society not to flatter my vanity or to humiliate them (I had other means of revenge, just admitting that I sought them out), but, as I said, because they were useful to me and because they circulated about Paris on my behalf. As for myself, I went to bed early. Thanks to them, I kept up with everything, the way Proust, from the depths of his bed, knew what had been said at all the dinners given the night before." Also: "Inasmuch as I seldom went out, it was essential that I be informed of everything that went on in the houses where my clothes were worn. I developed the habit, then unprecedented, of surrounding myself with people of quality so as to establish a link between myself and society. The Russian, Italian, and French aristocracy, English society women—all came and did service in the Rue

Cambon." Then Chanel added: "I have never paid idlers." Thus, it is clear that what might appear, at first glance, to be an assembly of parasites was in fact a group of well-known persons chosen and paid by a woman who, born of the people, was completely aware of the lacunae in her social history. The daughter of a Cévenole small-wares peddler counted on the sons of the nobility to initiate her into a style of life that was their birthright but, of course, not hers.

above In the foreground, Fulco (Duc di Verdura, Marquis Santostefano della Cerda) was a Sicilian, of very old family, who created remarkable jewelry for Chanel. Behind him: Don Guido Sommi Picenardi (Marquis di Calvetone), Baron Fabvier, and Count Étienne de Beaumont.

191

Chanel invents the unisex style

Putting women into slacks, made possible by the age's liberalization of morals and by the new opportunity in sports available to women of means, constituted the most spectacular of the innovations brought about by Chanel. It was she who gave this emulation of masculine attire its air of class, and it was she who adapted the style to every occasion, who subjected it to the demands of fashion and varied its interpretations, some sportive and casual, others elegant and refined. Wearing slacks in 1929 was, obviously, a freedom that only rich women could afford. Still, the taboo had been broken, and once the era of leisure and standardized clothing arrived, the Chanel mode had only to go down into the street for pants to become the preference of thousands upon thousands of

women. The photographs reproduced here, even though a half-century old, make one feel that the time of the all-purpose jean is near and that of the androgynous style too. Chanel anticipated those who today consider themselves innovative in their taste for work clothes, such as sailors' pullovers, dockworkers' T-shirts, and the white jackets traditional for plasterers. Before anyone else, she derived fashion from the netherworld of common man.

1 Gabrielle Chanel and her friend from younger days, the opera singer Marthe Davelli.
2 Chanel wearing a sailor shirt and wide pajamas made of jersey.
3 Chanel, jacketed and trousered in white duck, with the designer Lucien Lelong at Venice in 1931.

194

Chanel leaves her stamp on Saint-Moritz

The first PLM poster designed to promote winter sports appeared in 1900, the period when Switzerland and France were importing the first skis. The poster showed the lady skier dressed in an ankle-length skirt and low-heel shoes. One year before the outbreak of the Great War, Lartigue noted: "Winter sports are not very popular in France." But in the postwar era all this changed quite rapidly. More than any other sport, skiing was a luxury, and the resort that would offer the greatest luxury and at the earliest date was Saint-Moritz. It attracted the wealthy in great numbers from all nations.

1 In 1929 Chanel added to her *haute couture* collection a line of accessories made in wool jersey. Her matching caps and scarves were adopted by men (even though not made for them) just as quickly as they were by women, and put to use in a way never actually envisioned by Chanel—for winter sports.
2 The Comtesse Étienne de Beaumont, dressed like her sleighing companion and wearing a Chanel cap.
3–5 This series of photos shows Gabrielle Chanel at Saint-Moritz in the company of her friend and collaborator, Étienne de Beaumont. They are wearing the first ski togs: shoes that let in water and pants that twisted uncontrollably.
6 A toboggan party with the recognizable images of Maria Ruspoli, Duchesse de Gramont, Gabrielle Chanel, and Comtesse E. Moretti.

1929:
the "black lady"
of the Roaring Twenties
sets off
her last fireworks

1929: Taste was undergoing some kind of change. Not a decisive shift but a gradual one. At first hardly discernible, it became more pronounced during the social upheavals of 1936 and then continued at full speed until 1939. Yes, an age had passed. Gone since 1929 was the insolence of the first postwar years,

also the craze for black that had characterized both fashion and decoration. The decennials of taste have a way of fixing their own dates in the calendar. The Belle Époque did not open with the century, but in 1899, with the pardon granted to Captain Dreyfus, and ended not in 1910 but in 1914, with the guns of August. Correspondingly, the "Roaring Twenties" did not fall neatly into the 1920–30 decade usually assigned to them. Lanoux assures us: "The twenties. They are the ten years from the demobilization of 1919 to the 'crash' of 1929." Another bizarre thing is that while the new era would have a darker mood, fashion tended toward white.

the "white lady" of the thirties

Among the reminiscences of Chanel, as Morand reported them under the title *L'Allure de Chanel,* can be found these highly revealing lines concerning the origin of the vogue for white that suddenly seized the fashionable world in 1929: "I was the first to have rugs dyed beige. It reminded me of beaten earth. Right away furnishings all turned beige, until finally the decorators cried for mercy. 'Try white satin,' I said. Whereupon white swamped their ensembles. . . ." Chanel also noted that along with this search for "candid innocence and white satin" came a return to favor of Far Eastern brilliance, bringing white lacquer to walls, Chinese white to vitrines, pale rice paper to screens, and white flowers to vases.

In 1929, while the United States lived through September's "Black Friday," with its stock-market crash and bank closures, Paris, where the economy suffered less and the franc remained stable, entered a decade that for the *beau monde* would be incredibly luxurious, a time of splendid parties attended by women dressed in white satin. In her preface to the album that Horst entitled *Salute to the Thirties,* Janet Flanner called it "the unexpected apogee of France's rather dowdy Third Republic."

1 The whole style of the mad twenties—*les années folles*—had been decreed by Chanel: severe with a preference for black. But a change began to appear in 1926. No more tubular dresses. Slowly, between 1926 and 1929, clothes developed longer lines and greater flair. Here is Chanel's new black dress, as seen by *Vogue.*
2 Also in *Vogue,* a white dress of 1931. In Chanel's designs the magazine noted the "melon sleeve," a refinement upon a cut that was thought lost forever.
3 Drawing in *Vogue,* 1931. The great success of Chanel's collection, this dress is in white satin.

a veritable craze for satin

Everywhere satin. Simple or perverse, satin reigned at every level of society as the festive fabric of the thirties. It was in a mandarin costume made of white satin that the very beautiful and redoubtable Mrs. Reginald Fellowes, the era's famous hostess, received her guests at her *hôtel particulier* in Neuilly the evening of a sumptuous party: *Le Bal oriental*. And white satin was again the material when Madame Martinez de Hoz, a great South American beauty, appeared as Watteau's *Gilles* at the "Masterpiece Ball" given by Comte Étienne de Beaumont. Finally, dressed, gloved, and hatted in white satin, the indestructible Mistinguett, then well past sixty, had another triumph on the stage of the Folies-Bergère.

1 Drawing in *Vogue*, February 1930: an evening gown by Chanel.
2–3 Studies by Drian showing two views of a 1931 dress by Chanel that was most unusual for her. Although the wedding gown normally appeared as the ultimate "bouquet" or the finale of a collection, Chanel had always scorned the rite, declaring she wanted "no circus." Along with Eric, Benito, and Bouché, all of them foreigners, Drian, a lone Frenchman, was counted among the most gifted of the artists who drew dress models in the thirties.
4 Horst, photograph of the "Queen of Music Hall," Mistinguett, in *Folies en folies*.

America and England
assign their greatest photographers

Condé Nast, the owner of *Vogue* and *Vanity Fair*, begged Edward Steichen to replace Baron De Meyer, who had departed for the Hollywood studios. Steichen as much as Meyer, and probably in a more decisive way, had been the first to have a real effect on fashion photography, for he was the first to assimilate its style to that of avant-garde painting. Indeed, his influence went all the way back to 1900. The enormous salary offered to assure the services of Steichen had no precedent. But this master was quite simply the inventor of fashion photography as a profession and the first photographer to use professional models, such as Marion Morehouse. Signed in 1923, Steichen's contract lasted until 1938, the year that he abruptly gave up working in fashion. In 1947 Steichen became curator of the photography department at New York's Museum of Modern Art.

Writer and draftsman of genuine flair, theatre designer, ideal companion, adventurous traveler, witty conversationalist, a great and generous spirit, Cecil Beaton was a protean genius and, until his recent death, the last in a lost tradition, that of the great lords of fashion photography. This distinctively British man was also the quintessential cosmopolite. He belonged to Paris as much as to New York or even London, and was equally at home in his studio, where a tiny staff adored him, and at the English court, which he served as official portraitist. One of the master's most brilliant successes was the creation of the sets, costumes, and, especially, the hats for the Broadway production of *My Fair Lady*. In the realm of fashion photography, Beaton in 1925 perfected the studio technique of posing models against somewhat unreal or poetic environments, doing so with unique elegance.

1 Steichen, photograph for *Vogue*, 1930. Chanel used white organdy for this dress.

2 Sir Cecil Beaton, photograph for *Vogue*, 1935. Chanel used sequins and tulle.

Chanel poses for Iribe

1933: After twenty-three years of silence, an almost forgotten title, *Le Témoin*, reappeared on the kiosks of France. One might remember, however, that in its first incarnation of 1910 the journal had published an extraordinary caricature of Sarah Bernhardt, which served to introduce a new artist, Cocteau, who signed his work "Jim." In 1930, Iribe was again the director, editorial writer, and principal illustrator of the review, but this time with a publisher in the person of Chanel, who thereby exposed her affair with Iribe to a blaze of publicity. All Paris was talking about it. Iribe's drawing had lost nothing of its power, derived as it was from the same corrosive spirit and now, suddenly, exploited on behalf of the most blatant chauvinism. On every page, the sight of France and its *grandeur* maligned by the world—a Phrygian-capped personification placed in the dock before a sneering tribunal—was enough to rend the soul. But who were the judges? Chamberlain, Hitler, Mussolini, and Roosevelt! And in the guise of Marianne, this poor threatened France—this victim with her bare breast, half-buried under sod shoveled by a gravedigger named Daladier—bore an unmistakable resemblance to none other than Chanel.

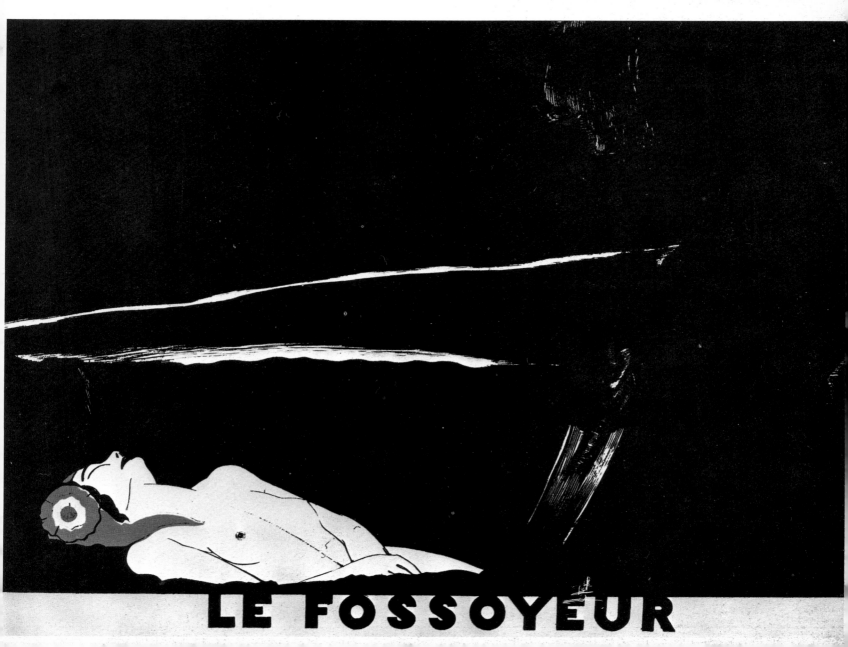

Coco's revenge

A frenzy of *fêtes,* marked by a lavishness never seen before,
seized high society in the years immediately preceding
World War II. The legendary Janet Flanner, Paris correspondent for the *New Yorker,* expressed amazement over
these manifestations of dazzling frivolity: "It was then that
in Paris a decade of private fêtes and splendid entertain-
ments began in the *beau monde.* . . . In their magnificently
furnished Paris mansions the *beau monde* had come into a
state of revival brought on by the national prosperity, all
the more welcome to them because of its contrast to their
previous state of ennui, the social dullness of the pinched
postwar years just passed." The "Oriental Ball," the "Circus Ball," the "Forest Ball," the "Masterpiece Ball," the
"Olympia Ball," etc. From May through July, lasting
from 1935 until the very height of the summer in 1939,
Paris saw an endless stream of masked balls.

At last recognized and invited everywhere, loved, and
according to public rumor, on the verge of marrying Iribe, was Chanel having her revenge and savoring it?

1   Sometimes, and no doubt without realizing it,
    Chanel revived the attitudes, graces, and coquetries
    of the *café-concert divette.* And seeing her in the
    costume that she made for Valentine Hugo on
    the occasion of the "Waltz Ball," one cannot
    help thinking of the young woman on the
    cover of the song that Chanel made
    her own during the period when
    she lit up the *beuglant* catering to
    the Moulins garrison.

2   Cover of *"Qui qu'a vu Coco?"*
    (see page 30).

3   Summer 1934. Chanel
    with Fulco di Verdura at the
    ball given by Prince Jean-Louis
    de Faucigny-Lucinge and Baron Ni-
    colas de Gunzburg.

204

as the war clouds gathered,

On January 4, 1935, Pierre Laval went to Rome to sign the Franco-Italian accords, while the French press hailed Mussolini and "his handsome peasant emperor's .head." But a few voices of a less lyrical sound could be heard, such as that of the Pope, who said to Ambassador Charles-Roux: "Mussolini tells us he is convinced that war will break out between the English and the Italians and then spread rapidly throughout Europe. He spoke of it all as if he were taking a cup of morning tea." Then there was Léon Blum in *Le Populaire:* "For the first time a French minister is a guest of the murderer of Matteoli. . . ." In fact, the agreement was signed only at the price of a debasement. What price? A free hand for Il Duce in Ethiopia. Rome rejoiced, for Fascist Italy could now pursue its war with no further delay. Less than a month later, a contingent of the Italian army set off for Ethiopia. When Haile Selassie, Menelik's grandson who had become Negus and then Emperor in 1930, saw his country thus threatened, he appealed for help to the League of Nations, a body the Ethiopian war would destroy. On October 3, 1935, Italy invaded Ethiopia, bringing Haile Selassie's denunciation of the bombings and the massacres of women and children. By May 3, 1936, the Italians had entered Addis Ababa. Soon, the war would take other turns and spread like wildfire to the rest of the world.

Paris rushed from party to party

In Paris the summer of 1935 was a time when Gabrielle Chanel, the gifted costume designer, and the stage designer Christian Bérard, whom fashionable women fought over for advice, were both dream merchants to a senseless society. They were the craftsmen of countless metamorphoses, the magicians of a shadowy theatre whose denizens spent the night until dawn pretending to be someone else.

But for Chanel 1935 also brought the summer when, one August day at La Pausa, Paul Iribe fell dead on the tennis court before her very eyes. With this she entered a long and cruel solitude.

1   As in every spring, 1935 saw the ball given by Count Étienne de Beaumont, who was by far the liveliest and most elegant person there. His theme this year? France's *Grand Siècle*—the Age of Louis XIV. Sergei Lifar attended as the dancer Vestris, wearing a costume made by Chanel.

2   The cover of a supplement to *L'Excelsior*. This special 36-page issue, illustrated with maps of Ethiopia and numerous photographs, appeared in October 1935, just when the League of Nations had voted to apply economic sanctions to Italy. Thus began Europe's gravest crisis since the end of World War I.

3   At Étienne de Beaumont's masked ball, Chanel impersonating Watteau's *Indifférent*.

1936: strike!

Spring 1936: In a country fraught with crisis, where severe poverty gripped the working class, where the price of grain fell to half that of 1929, where bankruptcies doubled, where unemployment continued to increase, a bitter election campaign got underway. But on April 26, 1936,

reported *L'Écho de Paris*. That relaxed, happy, and determined mood had the effect of a body blow. The second surprise came when the women joined the movement en masse, which left all observers in a state of indescribable stupefaction.

An unspeakable gesture—the staff at Chanel's went on strike. One June morning at opening time a smocked apprentice pasted a placard on the entrance announcing that the premises had been "occupied." Along with this was attached a standard cardboard box, decoratively tied with

passage. Chanel was on the steps of her own house, and her employees refused to obey her.

That women, by means of a strike, should seek to assert themselves in a country where salaries were outrageously low and job insecurity was total simply outraged Chanel, who would not tolerate such behavior. Thus, negotiations between Gabrielle and her staff began in a climate of high tension. She turned a deaf ear even to the most legitimate demands: employment contracts, weekly salaries, limited working hours, paid vacations. To that Chanel responded with the mass

the immense and resounding defeat of the right momentarily drowned out the noise over the German victory in the Saar plebiscite.

June 1936: "Inconceivable, unimaginable, inadmissable." Such were the terms with which *patrons* ("bosses") reacted to the wave of strikes that rolled across France in May. Soon, fear would be succeeded by—and the word is not too strong—terror. The explosion, which gathered force as it swelled, took on an unpredictable and thus doubly rebellious character. First of all there was the general atmosphere: "The good humor of the strikers is the most sinister of all the omens,"

ribbons but slit like a ballot box to permit the passing public to support the cause with contributions. Next, a group of *déléguées* appeared at the Ritz, where Chanel lived, and requested an audience with *la patronne*. Such a thing would have been unthinkable a fortnight before.

Mademoiselle let it be known that, being innocent of what a *déléguée* was, she could not receive one, but that she would see *her* workers in *her* own time at the Chanel salon. She dressed with care, putting on her triple-length rope of pearls, and presented herself at the portal of her *maison de couture*, where the delegates barred all

firing of three-hundred employees—who refused to budge. Things dragged on until her advisors indicated that if an agreement were not reached soon, there would be no hope of presenting an autumn collection. Finally, Mademoiselle gave in. This was undoubtedly one of the rare occasions in her long career when Gabrielle Chanel failed to conceal her deep consternation. Iribe was dead. Her business was all she had. She was alone in the world, alone in the face of rebellion.

1,2 Scenes during the strike at Chanel's.

Chanel/Visconti

A beautiful name, a splendid fortune, and a handsome physique. These were, when he met Chanel, the only assets of Luchino Visconti. In the circles where he moved, his passion for literature appeared most unusual. Moreover, he had a predilection for authors never heard of in his world. Scion of one of Italy's noblest families, the Visconti di Modrone, he seemed to embody a rather cruel contradiction. If aristocratic traditions, luxury, sumptuousness, and certain privileges remained incomparably fascinating for him, he was not any less sensitive to the causes of their inevitable disappearance. Even though he felt no sense of caste, the certainty of his class' decline obsessed him. And all the nobility to which Visconti had been born made him perceive this heritage as a "paradise lost," a feeling that was continually at odds with its possessor's desire for social justice.

Chanel conquered Visconti. He invited her to Italy and there presented her to his father, who also fell under the Frenchwoman's charm. And it was at the height of the Popular Front that Gabrielle succeeded in persuading Jean Renoir to allow Luchino Visconti to watch him make a film. Renoir was then working on *Les Bas-Fonds* ("The Lower Depths"), based upon the play by Maxim Gorky and starring Jean Gabin and Louis Jouvet, after having finished *La Vie est à nous*, a propaganda film commissioned by the Communist Party. Renoir not only accepted into the studio the presence of an Italian aristocrat with the bearing of a *condottiere*, but, shortly thereafter, even took him on as an assistant. And it was with him that Renoir made *Une Partie de campagne*, thereby opening the doors of a future for Visconti.

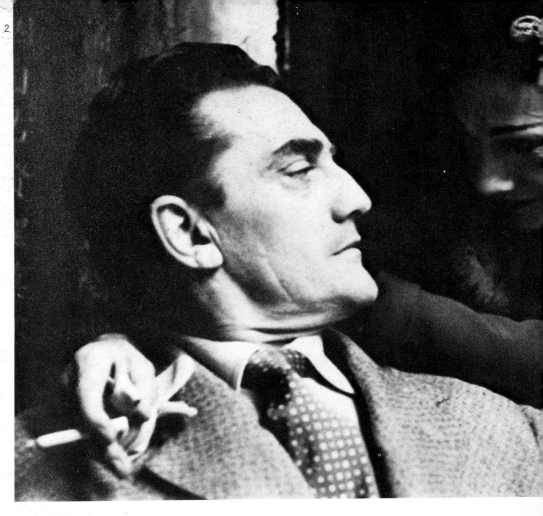

Chanel/Renoir

It was the day after Munich that Renoir, still glowing from the success of *La Grande Illusion*, approached Chanel and asked her to do the costumes for his next film. "We are going to try to make a gay picture. This has been a life-long ambition of mine," declared Renoir. What emerged was *La Règle du jeu* ("The Rules of the Game"). The subject? An upper-class woman deceived by her husband. Would she in turn be unfaithful to him and with whom? The drama develops when the heroine is courted by a famous aviator of modest means, for the rule of this occult game is that members of the aristocracy may not ally themselves with anyone from without. But the rule must be applied suavely; thus, the intruder will be shot like a rabbit by a jealous gamekeeper. A fortuitous accident allowing the murder to be judged inadvertent and the whole affair smoothed over. Chanel's costumes expressed to perfection what was a cruel paraphrase of *Les Caprices de Marianne*, a scathing image of château life in the 1930s. Now Chanel found herself linked to the fate of Renoir's most ambitious and pessimistic film, a sublimely witty performance that marked the climax of his achievement—and the turning point in its creator's life. Not only was the picture booed, it was even banned. In 1939, the year the film appeared, the military censors deemed it "demoralizing." Disgusted, Renoir left France forever and took up residence in the United States.

1 Luchino Visconti in 1936.
2 Visconti and Gabrielle Chanel in 1938.
3 Jean Renoir, actor, with Nora Grégor in *La Règle du jeu*. Costumes by Chanel, 1939.

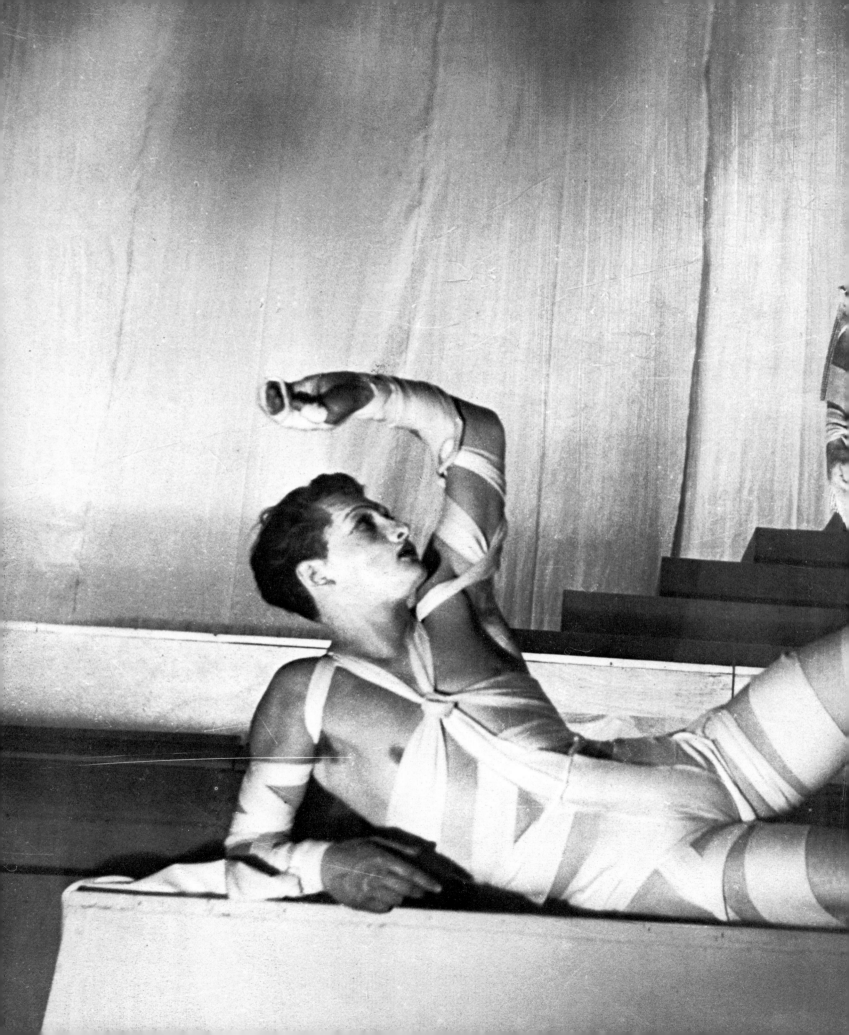

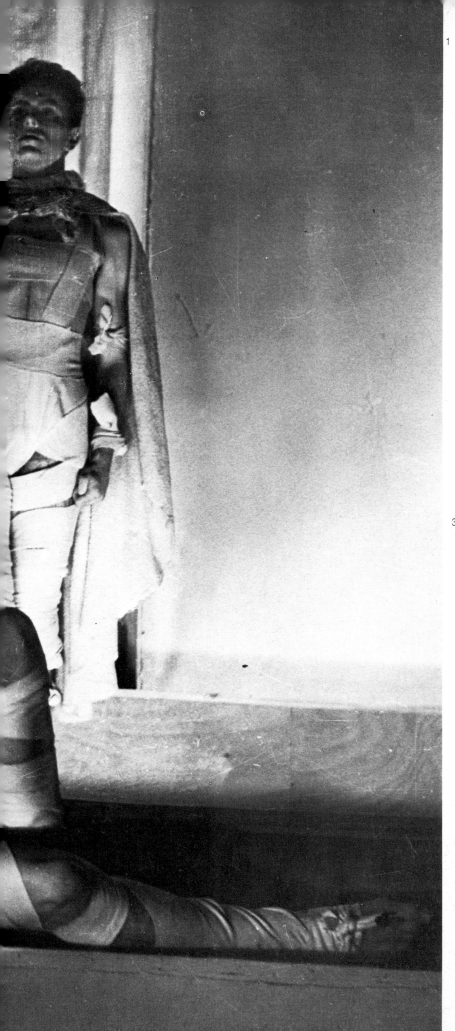

for *Oedipus Rex*, costumes that created a scandal

In 1937 designing for the theatre continued to occupy Chanel, as it did without interruption until the declaration of war, undoubtedly because, of all her tasks, this one proved most effective in dispelling her loneliness and depression. Jean Cocteau dominated the theatre, fashion, and taste of Paris in these years. And since it was from Cocteau that a group of young, unknown actors wanted an adaptation of *Oedipus Rex,* an ancient drama never before given in modern times, Chanel received the commission for costumes. She responded with a strange interlacement of mummy-like wrappings, which the critics found to be of a rare indecency.

1   The debut of an unknown: Jean Marais.
2   Cocteau, drawing of Chanel in a Chanel.
3   Iya Abdy, a Russian of great beauty, was a member of the *Oedipus Rex* company. For a necklace, she wore spools of thread all strung together.

the two rivals

The thirties saw the rise of a new prima donn[a] of *haute couture*. This was Elsa Schiaparelli, a Ro[man] man lady of a well-to-do family that had pro[duced] duced such illustrious men of learning as a grea[t] astronomer, for whom a street in Rome wa[s] named, and an archaeologist who had locate[d] the site of the first tomb in Egypt's Valley of th[e] Kings. But not only was Elsa a person of soli[d] background, she also had a lively intelligenc[e] and native originality, all of which endowed he[r] work with a quality as mad as it was provocative[.] By bringing a new tone to elegance, she threat[ened] ened the primacy of Chanel. Soon the compet[i] tion between the two women would become a[n] unremitting vendetta. As her clients, Schiap[arelli]

...elli began with only a small group of women who, far from wishing to promote her talent, preferred to remain the only ones who knew the address of that ingenious individual whose little sweaters were the most amusing in Paris. But when in 1927 *Vogue* decided to name a Schiaparelli sweater "the sweater of the year," the magazine launched the designer upon a great career.

Chanel, still smarting from Madeleine Vionnet's habit of calling her "that milliner," would always refer to Schiaparelli as "the Italian," and never once pronounced her name.

photos Horst, portraits of the two rivals in 1936.

215

23 Schiaparelli

1

1936

21 Chanel

Chanel
Taffetas noir

Schiaparelli
Tweed bleu-marine

Bérard

2

a remorseless duel

The competition had an Italian name: Schiaparelli. Until 1933 Chanel proceeded largely unchallenged. Parisian *haute couture*, like high fashion, constituted an empire in which the power was held by women—women of great renown, such as Vionnet, Lanvin, Alix, Louise Boulanger, and the Callot sisters. Each of them had her following. Now there arrived on the scene a highly creative individual whose taste was directly opposed to Chanel's but who nonetheless attracted the same kind of woman. Schiaparelli too enjoyed glamorous friendships. Indeed, her embroideries were conceived by Salvador Dali. And she reinforced her cause from surprising quarters. Thus, her necklaces were the work not of some Grand Duchess (which by then would hardly have been original) but by a young Russian much admired by *le Tout-Montparnasse*. She too was called Elsa, and her lover, a certain Aragon, the poet, took charge of Schiaparelli's deliveries. He could be found running up and down the stairs *chez* "Schiap," his arms loaded with female finery. In sum, the friend of the Surrealists was now taking on the friend of the Cubists. The fashion press, which gleefully reported the beginnings of

the sort of confrontation that has always delighted Paris, increasingly compared Schiap's dresses with those of Chanel. In order to please the publications quarreling over which side he favored, Christian Bérard, who had just attained glory with his costumes and sets for Cocteau's *La Machine infernale*, divided his time and talents as best he could between the two rivals.

1   Schiaparelli and Chanel dresses drawn by Bérard for *Vogue* in 1936 and 1937.
2   Chanel in 1938 with her stable of mannequins, all coiffed like *la patronne* and dressed by her in elegant smocks.
3   Maurice Sachs, after observing Chanel as she followed the fashion show from behind her mirrors, described the *couturière* in his *Decade of Illusion:* "She was like a general, one of those young Napoleonic generals possessed by a will to win."
4   "It is Chanel who made it all possible," Cocteau wrote to Jouvet. She had persuaded Popesco to produce Cocteau's *La Machine infernale*, with direction by Louis Jouvet. Here she is in 1934, a vision of beauty and success.

a court of
portrait photographers

At age fifty-five, Gabrielle Chanel was in the prime of her beauty. Her features, like her figure, had reached their ultimate refinement. And never had she dressed with more invention or with greater perfection. Never had she been more admired, or more invited. Making an appearance became an obligation, for she had to show herself in order to deal with the competition. Elsa Schiaparelli was hard on her heels. Chanel decided to create and reign over a veritable court of photographers. They proved to be more than interested in her face: they were passionate about it.

1 George Hoyningen-Huene, Gabrielle Chanel in 1935. This extraordinary portrait of Chanel stands apart from all other known images of her. Is it because of the contrast between the modernity of the face and the classically Spanish look of the lace ruff? At the time of this picture, Hoyningen-Huene, a

thirty-five-year-old Russian aristocrat, had made a modest start as a designer for a small dressmaking concern owned by his sister and had even attempted to paint in the manner of André Lhote. Then he came to the notice of Edna Chase, the close collaborator of the all-powerful Condé Nast, the publisher of *Vogue*. Once engaged in 1925 as the permanent Paris representative of the American *Vogue*, he soon emerged as one of the principal stars of that publication. Hoyningen-Huene was a curious man, sometimes exploding with imagination, then sometimes sinking into a deep melancholy. Born in St. Petersburg of a Baltic baron and an American mother, he was consumed by a veritable passion for France and Paris. But when war broke out, he became convinced that Europe was finished forever. By 1946 this quintessential European had taken up residence in Hollywood, where he spent his time as a color coordinator for George Cukor and other film directors and as a photography teacher. There he died in 1968.
2–3 Sir Cecil Beaton, two portraits of Gabrielle Chanel made in her home c. 1935.

at the center of the artistic life of her time

1 Les Ballets de Monte-Carlo, supported by American financiers, beneficiary of patronage from the principality of Monte Carlo, and directed by René Blum, was the only dance company that came to the aid of Diaghilev's troupe. By 1932 it could boast the presence of a number of dancers formerly with the Ballets Russes, along with Diaghilev's choreographers and collaborators, among others Alexandra Danilova, Woizikovski, Kochno, Balanchine, and Massine. In 1938 Monte Carlo witnessed the creation of Massine's choreography for Beethoven's Seventh Symphony, with designs by Christian Bérard, as well as Massine's *La Gaieté parisienne*, danced against sets by Étienne de Beaumont. It was a triumphant season.

After the opening, celebrities gathered at a supper given by Prince de Faucigny-Lucinge. Left to right: Alexandra Danilova, who starred in *La Gaieté parisienne*, Salvador Dali, Gabrielle Chanel, and Georges Auric.

2   May 1938: In the wings of the Théâtre de l'Athénée, following the dress rehearsal of a play by Marcel Achard, *Le Corsaire*, which Louis Jouvet directed and Christian Bérard designed, Gabrielle Chanel congratulates Jouvet. Notable features of her attire are the heavy white crepe of the dress and the mixture of real and fake jewelry.

3   Photograph in *Vogue*. Here, in October 1938, Chanel made a stunning entrance at André Durst's "Forest Ball" dressed like a tree and wearing black face powder.

4   Chanel and Christian Bérard were photographed in the Italian Pavilion the day it was inaugurated in 1937 at the Paris Exposition des Arts et Techniques.

5   After the dress rehearsal of *Le Corsaire*, during a supper given by Misia Sert, Marie-Laure de Noailles, Igor Stravinsky, Vera de Bosset Sudeikin, whom the composer would marry in 1940, and Gabrielle Chanel.

such was fashion during the last summer of dancing

1938. Chanel's prestige had never been higher. The *couturière* suffered no damage from the competition offered by Schiaparelli; indeed, she met it point for point. When her rival launched, to great fanfare, a new color—"shocking pink"—Chanel introduced her irresistibly seductive gypsy style. It ravished America, along with the best of French and foreign artists, whose drawings appeared to great effect in all the magazines.

"In Paris, *le sex-appeal* is the principal theme of all the new collections," the English edition of *Vogue* noted with satisfaction, adding that for daytime the waist was in and well cinched, whereas for evening everything was fire and flames, thanks to the craze for sequins, which proliferated all over bodices, boleros, and skirt bottoms. Finally, one read that the hats were all perfectly ridiculous, with the exception of those made of faille ribbons, and these were the last word in chic. But however brilliant the fashion, it would have a brief life.

Once war had been declared in 1939, all such frippery disappeared. Meanwhile, the neat and attractive daytime wear of that year endured, practically unchanged, throughout the occupation, as if in that ungrateful period fashion wanted to preserve the happy impression of Europe's last moment of peace.

1 Bérard, drawing in *Vogue*, 1937. While Schiaparelli was cutting off slacks at mid-calf, Chanel persisted in her objection to anything that did not fall in a straight line like the classic suit worn by men. Here a black, belted blouse, with pants and jacket in printed cotton.
2 Bouché, sketch in *Vogue*, 1938. Gypsy dresses by Chanel.
3 Pagès, drawing in *Vogue*, 1938. A hat made of blue faille ribbon, a short Bertha cape (like the *pèlerines* of Gabrielle's girlhood), and gloves by Chanel.
4 Eric, drawing in the French edition of *Vogue*, 1939. A *tricolore* number, the last evening dress presented by Gabrielle Chanel before the declaration of war and the closing of her house.

223

elegance for what?

From 1940 to 1941, a time when everyone thought Hitler would win the war, a certain contingent of *le Tout-Paris* joined the collaboration as if it were the natural thing to do. In Fabre-Luce's *Journal de la France* one could read: "The green uniform is, after all, the latest novelty that Paris, in its *natural* curiosity and frivolity, is trying to tame."

1   A Parisian openly flirting with "the latest novelty."

2   The curfew was imposed with the greatest strictness. At eleven o'clock theatregoers and night owls caught the last Métro. Here is Fréhel, the *chanteuse* whose realist repertoire appealed to the German audience.

3   At the Pigalle Métro station, she who was still only *la môme* Piaf.

4   A German officer shared Chanel's life during and after the Occupation. Here he is before the war, at a time when he called himself an embassy attaché, but in fact was in Paris as the director of propaganda for the Reich. His name: Hans Gunther von Dincklage.

5   Chanel at the opening of an exhibition of paintings by Cassandre. With her is Lifar who at the Opéra dominated the world of dance. Received by Hitler, he had been proposed by Göring, in anticipation of a German victory, as director of the future European Ballet.

6   The Nazi flag flying over the Ritz, which had been completely requisitioned by the Germans. Chanel managed not to be thrown out of her room.

haute couture
or whom?

With the exception of Chanel, who closed her salon immediately after war was declared, the *couturiers* of Paris went right on presenting two collections a year. Wool and silk had disappeared, but even with ersatz materials, *haute couture* worked wonders.

Elegance c. 1941. A full-skirted coat permitted the wearer to travel by bicycle. Completing the ensemble were a shoulder-strap bag, a shopping basket on the handle-bars, low boots with imitation felt and cork soles, and a hat enveloped in a cloud of veiling.

No restrictions for the milliners, who were exempted from textile rationing. Illustrated is a wartime creation by Jeannette Colombier.

In 1942 the *haute couture* trade association decided to take the spring collections to the Free Zone for presentation, not only to German and Italian buyers but also to Swiss and Spanish ones. Shown here is the arrival of the star designers: Jeanne Lanvin, Marcel Rochas, and Jacques Fath.

0 *Mannequins* and *vendeuses* en route to Lyons.

1 The mannequin's compartment in the Part-Dieu Station. Sleeping cars served as their hotel. Note the crucifix next to *Signal*, the anglophobic, anti-Semitic, anti-bolshevik daily that had a circulation of 420,000.

2 The fashion show at the Théâtre des Célestins.

3 Jacques Fath at work.

4 With baubles lent by the best of Parisian jewelers, the police kept a close watch.

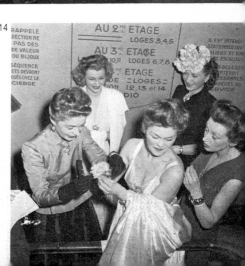

a trap signed Avedon

For some two weeks after that historic morning on August 26, 1944—when General de Gaulle and leaders of the Resistance marched under a brilliant sun from the Arc de Triomphe to Notre-Dame, sometimes to the roar of applause, sometimes to the crack of gunfire—order in Paris remained an agonizing problem and the danger of insurrection very great. How could it have been otherwise in a city left to itself, where the police now found themselves identified with the dispossessed, where those formerly in authority were now destitute and often under arrest, where the new authority had not yet gained credibility, where—worst of all—undesirable elements had introduced themselves into the ranks of the insurgents and, under the guise of resistance, were in the process of settling personal accounts.

It was in the dark atmosphere of summary executions and kangaroo courts that Chanel was apprehended in September of 1944. Many years later she would still all but choke with fury when recalling the day two men arrived at the Ritz and unceremoniously demanded that she follow them forthwith. The order for her arrest came from the Committee of Public Morals. One can imagine the alarm that ran through her entourage. But a few hours later Chanel was released and allowed to return to the Ritz. Thus, it must be said that relative to what was inflicted upon those who had embraced a policy of collaboration, or to what popular wrath imposed upon women who had become romantically involved with Germans, Gabrielle experienced a very slight hell. She was not paraded nude through the streets, nor was her head shaved and her brow marked with a swastika. Shortly thereafter, moreover, Chanel managed to reach Switzerland without difficulty. She would remain there eight years, an exile who returned to France only for brief visits. Then, less than two years later, she was even permitted to go to the United States. This was indeed surprising, because for a very long time, visa re-quests for America received the most careful scrutiny. Chanel, however, had no more problem making this new trip in 1947 than she had had in going to Switzerland in 1945. Obviously, protection from a very high source had assured her a liberty that others, a good deal less culpable than she, did not enjoy. The day after Liberation, an order transcending all debate had with one firm stroke kept her from being purged. To whom did she owe this impunity? It is thought, although without absolute confirmation, that it was the intervention of the Duke of Westminster with his friend Winston Churchill which made Chanel the beneficiary of an indulgence and a consideration known to no other person in those troubled days.

photo A trap signed Avedon. In 1948 a young American photographer was beginning to make a reputation for himself. For the second time his reports on the Paris collections, published in *Harper's Bazaar*, had, quite rightly, been judged both innovative and important. The young man in question attended the fashion shows, still as a statue, at the side of his formidable editor-in-chief, Carmel Snow. He was Richard Avedon, and he took advantage of his trip to Paris to look up Chanel. She was then making a brief stop in the Rue Cambon, a figure tragically on the sidelines of everything. There were many who, resentful of her wartime behavior, refused to speak to the great *couturière*. Chanel lived as if in quarantine, which made her all the more happy to see the foreign photographer who appeared and asked her to pose for him. Avedon had found a wall pasted over with two posters that, because of their association with Chanel, constituted one of those telling contrasts for which he already knew the secret. Chanel, without suspecting the trap that this pitiless young man had set for her, posed in front of the wall. But then Avedon had the tact not to release this eloquent portrait drama during her life.

Bérard

Christian Dior
La ligne corolle
Jaquette cintrée en shantung,
jupe longue finement plissée.

1947:
the Dior bombshell

On February 12, 1947, during a glacial, coal-starved winter, a forty-two-year-old designer (whom only a few knew as the *modéliste* at Lelong from 1942 to 1946)—a rank newcomer named Dior—presented to a wonderstruck audience a series of creations that would revolutionize every principle of modern dress for women. The continuing prewar style—with its skirt length fixed just below the knee, its straight lines accentuating neither the hips nor the bust, its padded shoulders, all dating from 1939 and adapted to conditions imposed by the Occupation—disappeared in one stroke. Skirts dropped 20 centimeters to a level below the calf. Shoulders not only shed their squareness and padding but actually became as soft and delicate as possible. Straight lines were replaced by a wasp waist that set off the bust, which, like the hips, assumed a fullness that skillful stiffening emphasized still further. From these changes came the silhouette the English-speaking press immediately dubbed the "New Look," signifying the "womanly woman" (*femme-femme*), a look launched by Christian Dior in an atmosphere of excitement and enthusiasm, generated by the professionalism of the work, the perfect cutting and finish of the clothes, the sheer wealth of material (some 15 meters for a daytime dress, 25 for an evening gown), and the rustle of rediscovered petticoats. Also contributing to the euphoria was the devastating beauty of the mannequins, who accepted the stupefaction they aroused with aloof, almost absent-minded expressions, sweeping along whole ranks of spectators as if by the very grace of their movements and gestures they could dispel all the gloom of the postwar period, that time of rationed milk, bread, wine, and sugar, of chronic strikes and soaring inflation.

The Paris papers were on strike the day after the birth of the New Look, with the result that the bomb first exploded abroad, where it became front-page news. Dior had an instantaneous success, which brought a veritable tidal wave of buyers and individual clients into the

Avenue Montaigne. And success arrived despite the reactions of certain American interests eager to save, by means of hostile articles, inventories worth millions, which the New Look would nonetheless render obsolete. Women's organizations in the United States even called on Dior to cease his "indecencies."

In England Sir Stafford Crips, the Minister of Economic Affairs, expressed indignation and insisted that the country maintain a short-skirt style conforming to common sense and the rigorous restrictions still in effect. But all such efforts proved futile, for when the French Ambassador to London held a private showing, the two royal Princesses themselves applauded the works of Christian Dior, almost in unison with France's commerce minister and the man-in-the-street, all of whom rejoiced over the triumph of *le nioulouk*.

1 Christian Bérard, sketch of a suit by Dior.
2 In a gray salon with Proustian decorations, a timid unknown, surrounded by his staff of female directors, prepares his collection: Christian Dior.

the return
of an old lady

1954: Dior's triumph could only make Chanel seem all the more forgotten. It simply confirmed the fact that a radical change had taken place and that nothing could bridge the gap left by such a long absence. Whereas prewar couture had been entirely dominated by women— Lanvin, Schiaparelli, Vionnet, Alix—it now fell into the hands of men—Balenciaga, Dior, Piguet, Fath, among others. It was an ineluctable revolution, and Chanel, whose couture house had been closed for fifteen years, felt herself afloat in an endless "off season." The more Dior's star gained ascendancy, the more Chanel's sank into obscurity.

Still, slowly, the conviction grew within Chanel that the time was approaching when women would be seized by a furious desire to throw off those waist cinchers, padded bras, heavy skirts, and stiffened jackets. Astonishingly, she even judged the right moment. By 1953 Gabrielle had made her decision and now began work, with the idea of reopening her salon the following year. She was more than seventy years old.

1 Gabrielle Chanel, who ten years later would find a new fountain of youth in her work, returned to Paris a terribly changed woman. In her little black jacket and utterly plain skirt, she seemed almost provincial. All that remained from the Chanel of yore was the obvious and undeniable severity of her taste.

231

a controversial reopening

On February 5, 1954, the mood in the Rue Cambon prior to the opening of Chanel's first postwar collection resembled that of a courtroom in the final minutes before a verdict. A throng of journalists from Italy, Germany, the United States, and England had filled the front-row seats next to those taken by the French press, and together all those women constituted a kind of tribunal. But where was the defendant? Many of her clients had come to see Chanel, who, however, remained in her favorite place, hidden away and invisible at the top of the stairs, seated on the final step where the mirrors permitted her to see everything without being seen. She had consciously chosen the fifth day of the month, for 5 had been her lucky number ever since 1921, when she had given it to *Chanel No. 5,* the perfume of perfumes and the foundation upon which her prodigious fortune had been built over the years (amounting to some $15 million, if one can believe the figures published by *Time* in 1971).

But this precaution did nothing to change the verdict of the critics, who voted for capital punishment. One writer, Michel Déon, now a member of the French Academy, attended that memorable reopening at the side of Chanel. He recalled it in an article published in *Les Nouvelles littéraires*: "The French press were atrocious in their vulgarity, meanness, and stupidity. They drubbed away at her age, assuring everyone that she had learned nothing in fifteen years of silence. We watched the mannequins file by in icy silence." The headlines of the daily papers had a field day. *Combat:* "At Chanel's it's Fouilly-les-Oies" (meaning way out in the sticks); *L'Aurore:* "A melancholy retrospective." The English dailies were hardly less ferocious. "A fiasco" was how the *Daily Mail* began its story. And if anything hurt Gabrielle, it was, undoubtedly, the brusque and violent public contempt displayed by her English friends.

232

the Chanel "look" goes down into the streets

1954: The day after what the English-language press called a "comeback," Chanel's ability was doubted, and in the final analysis, her reopening had to be written off as a devastating loss. Moreover, the designer herself agreed that after fifteen years of inactivity she had lost her touch. Still worse was the anxiety felt by her business associates, who feared that the negative publicity might end by affecting the sales of the Chanel perfumes.

It took Chanel a year to regain her full powers, but much sooner than that the signs of a rapid recovery began to appear in the United States. Contrary to all expectations, the dresses presented at the reopening—those dresses that had been so severely criticized by the press that the clothing manufacturers were kicking themselves for having counted on the prestige of the Chanel name—these very dresses were in fact selling better than anyone had imagined they might. Seventh Avenue watched with unbelieving eyes.

What was happening? American women were voting in vast numbers for the clothes of a designer whom a knowing public was calling "Coco." Now it all began again, and in France as well. Chanel had once more changed the way women dress and imposed her style on the streets themselves.

1 The Chanel "look," *Vogue*, 1954.
2 The fervent support of the popular magazines, and especially the weekly *Elle*.

the reconquest of an empire

At the second collection presented by Chanel, *Life*, then the most widely read of all the American magazines, took up the case of that very elderly lady who, after a struggle, had regained the premier position in the *haute couture* market. *Life* agreed that the celebrated *couturière* had miscalculated when she made her precipitate return, but so great had her influence already become that Chanel seemed to have initiated less a fashion than a revolution.

When asked to explain her victory, Chanel articulated ideas that were essentially very simple: "A garment must be logical." And this was what she aimed for. In her view, the creations of *ces messieurs*—by which she meant her male competitors—were the very opposite of logical: "Ah no, definitely no, men were not meant to dress women." But she allowed the men a role, even a determining one: it was them that women had to please.

1 Irving Penn, a famous photograph in *Vogue*, 1960. Allure in the Chanel manner, elegance with comfort, true style, the reflection of an era.
2 Frances McLaughlin, photographs made for *Vogue*, 1956. A pair of classic Chanels: a black suit lined in white and a dress in black *mousseline de soie*.

the maxims of Chanel— what she thought about life, love, women, and her profession

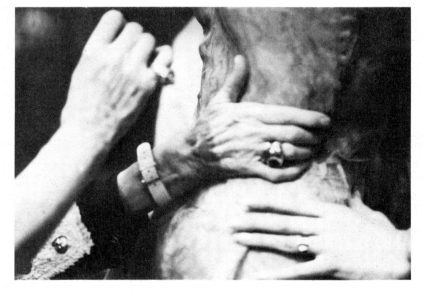

It is said that women dress for other women, and out of a spirit of competition. This is true. But if there were no longer any men, women would no longer dress at all.

"Good taste" ruins certain real values of the spirit: taste itself, for instance.

Fashion has two purposes: comfort and love. Beauty comes when fashion succeeds.

An elegant woman should be able to do her marketing without making housewives laugh. Those who laugh are always right.

Costume designers work with a pencil: it is art. *Couturiers* with scissors and pins: it is a news item.

Sem said to me, concerning some jewelry that I had designed: "At last we imitate the fake." How right he was. It is impossible to wear lots of real jewels unless there are women who wear lots of fake ones.

It is in paintings or in family albums that traces of true fashion are to be found.

Coquetry, it's a triumph of the spirit over the senses.

True generosity means accepting ingratitude.

The time comes when one can do nothing further to a work; this is when it has reached its worst.

Comfort has forms. Love has colors. A skirt is made for crossing the legs and an armhole for crossing the arms.

Fashion is at once both caterpillar and butterfly. Be a caterpillar by day and a butterfly by night. Nothing could be more comfortable than a caterpillar and nothing more made for love than a butterfly. There must be dresses that crawl and dresses that fly. The butterfly does not go to market, and the caterpillar does not go to a ball.

To disguise oneself is charming: to have oneself disguised is sad.

Fashion does not exist unless it goes down into the streets. The fashion that remains in the salons has no more significance than a costume ball.

Adornment, what a science! Beauty, what a weapon! Modesty, what elegance!

For a woman, to deceive makes only one kind of sense: that of the senses.

Make the dress first, not the embellishment.

A dress is not a dressing. It is made to be worn. One wears clothes with the shoulders. A dress should hang from the shoulders.

One day I heard an old seamstress saying to a young seamstress: "Never a button without a buttonhole." This simple and admirable statement could serve as a motto for *couturiers* and also for architects, musicians, and painters.

A failed innovation is painful: revival of it is sinister.

Fashion should slip out of your hands. The very idea of protecting the seasonal arts is childish. One should not bother to protect that which dies the minute it is born.

A beautiful dress may look beautiful on a hanger, but that means nothing. It must be seen on the shoulders, with the movement of the arms, the legs, and the waist.

Our houses are our prisons: let us learn how to liberate ourselves in the way we arrange them.

One can get used to ugliness, but never to negligence.

Fashion is always a reflection of its own time, but we forget this if it is stupid.

Nature gives you the face you have at twenty; life shapes the face you have at thirty; but at fifty, you get the face you deserve.

If you were born without wings, do nothing to prevent their growing.

Luxury is a necessity that begins where necessity ends.

1 Gabrielle Chanel at eighty during the final fitting of a collection dress.
2 The hands of Chanel. She said: "Much seriousness is required to achieve the frivolous."

backstage

Once she had regained her primacy, Chanel reigned over couture, from her seventy-ninth year to her eighty-eighth, a solitary figure, respected, proud, and always tyrannical. She lived only for her work, and the passion that she brought to it was the secret of her appeal, an elixir washing away the bitterness of exile and forced inactivity.

Throughout the final days and nights prior to the first showing of each collection, the great designer had the model dresses brought from the workrooms by the tailors and forewomen so that she could inspect them one by one. This took place in the vast mirror-lined salon where the public would crowd in on opening day. A few carefully chosen intimates were allowed to attend Gabrielle Chanel during these exhausting nights, but in silence and from a distance. The mannequins would come forth from the secrecy of the atelier, tall ambulatory figures, and make their appearance with all the submissiveness of conscripts. They had to endure interminable fittings without uttering a syllable, knowing only too well that Chanel would have remained deaf to their protests, deaf also to their fatigue and that of the tailors, while yet again she undid a jacket, cutting the stitches of an armhole that she would then redo right on the mannequin, using pins to reposition it point by point, all stuck in with an almost demonic thrust—and equally deaf to everything but the creative process that slowly was leading toward perfection. Her face tense, she scrutinized the work and, spotting a suspected bulge, seized upon the defect with fingers like tentacles. She would smoothe and shape the material, for the flaw had to be eliminated. Finally satisfied, she would sit down, fainting with exhaustion. After taking a swallow of water, she might well say abruptly to a friend there: "What ever are you looking at?" Then on to the next fitting. At last, her associates had to give up and leave her alone, well past midnight and still struggling, sometimes as humble and touching as an old artisan, but often aggressive, sure of herself, and restless, armed as she was with her long and powerful scissors, which she carried either at her belt like a sword, or around her neck like some mysterious order of knighthood.

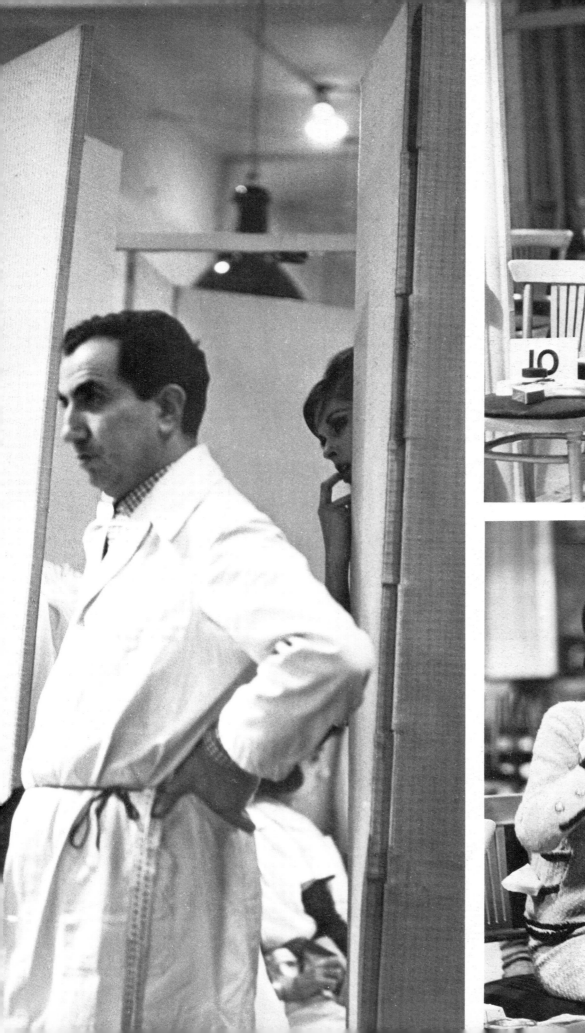

the rite

The place was vast and seemed in no way commercial, enhanced as it was with tall windows, the teasing reflections of mirror-glazed panels, and the array of Coromandel screens that, opened out, stood around a stage, forming a sort of little theatre.

Arranged upon chairs were trays filled with necklaces, flowers, brooches, chains, and belts—embellishments ready to be selected but only in the final stage, after all the fittings of the model dress had been finished. The moment the person in charge of accessories made a discreet appearance, the sign had come that the final touch would be applied. And in reality, when Chanel with both hands took the hat extended to her—more often than not a variation upon her favorite theme, the straw boater that she began with, the success that had launched her in that distant time when she was merely the clandestine love, the anonymous mistress of Étienne Balsan—and placed it on the head of the mannequin, pulling the form straight down and then making certain it sat securely upon the brow, the whole occasion assumed the quality of a rite. Then came the moment when, her creation having been refined, corrected, and concluded, Chanel—with that movement of a painter before his easel—stood back to see the fruits of her labor, all the while talking to herself: "Now . . . there you are . . . it's not so tacky, is it? Not too bad, don't you think? *Allez!*" This authorized the mannequin to take the ultimate pose on the podium between the Coromandel screens, for a viewing there just in case. . . . And if no alarm sounded¡ if she was not assaulted by a peremptory voice, the mannequin disappeared into the wings. The fitting was over.

pages 334–335 *Le défilé*: The press showing took place without flowers or music. Nothing written either, no printed statement placed on the chairs in order to reveal the secret intentions of the designers whose work they were about to judge, no program, no lyrical preface, for the simple reason that the mistress of this house had a horror of that sort of thing. She heaped sarcasm on all her competitors who had recourse to what she called *la poésie couturière*. Nothing of that at her place. Moreover, she had been the first to abandon the practice of giving names to her dresses. Her mannequins came out from the dressing room looking absolutely calm. They made their appearance in a paddock of mirrors, without winking, without provocative hip swings, and without dancing or smiling. Seated all in a row (see the following two pages), the major clients were the first to judge. Afterwards came the reporters' turn. The mannequins walked down the line—made their *défilé*—carrying a placard marked with a number, "like jockeys astride their own horses," wrote Jean Cocteau; "provided with a registration number, like convicts," said Paul Morand.

"It's because couture is not theatre, and fashion is not an art, it's a craft." This was Chanel's view.

the gestures and movements of life

Invention, talent, perfectionism, perseverence, and a vast capacity for hard work—none of it suffices to explain the power that Chanel had over women, fashion, and the artists of her time, nor why that power was so absolute. She had, it is true, a sacred account to settle with society, and possessed the "kind of solid appetite for vengeance that revolutions are made of," as Morand so rightly said. But even this cannot entirely explain or significantly clarify the mystery of such power, especially if at some moment in her career, after this had been crowned with success, the spirit of revenge subsided. Actually, it never did. On the contrary, the feeling became, if anything, more determined each time she detected in her midst some desire for a return to the past. She hated everything that, by reducing women to the status of objects, had for so long inhibited their ability to keep pace with men. Throwing off the shackles was her key obsession and her fixed objective. It thus became essential that a skirt and jacket serve and, if possible, encourage the movements and gestures of modern life: walking, running, sudden sitting down and getting up. She condemned without appeal and with utter ferocity anything that seemed to favor the taste of another time. That a *couturier* should have recourse to whalebone, corsets, and petticoats was enough to make her explode with rage: "Was he mad, this man? Was he making fun of women? How, dressed in 'that thing,' could they come and go, live or anything? . . ." Live! Here was the need that gave birth to the Chanel style, the style that was her sole pride: "I don't like people talking about the Chanel fashion," she said. "Chanel—above all else, it is a style. Fashion, you see, goes out of fash-

ion. Style never." To the end of her life, Chanel remained accessible and delighted whenever talented young artists sought her out for help and advice. It was to Chanel, we should not forget, that Alain Resnais went for the stunning costumes that Delphine Seyrig wore in *Last Year at Marienbad*.

1 Visconti introduced Chanel to Romy Schneider, who landed in Paris a mixture of child and star. Visconti, playing Svengali, was testing her abilities through the tragedy *Dommage qu'elle soit une p. . . .* One can still recall the grandeur of that much-discussed spectacle, which brought to the stage the atmosphere of a murderous nursery. Romy was already giving the lie to those Parisians who predicted that she would forever remain a prisoner of Sissy's Viennese mannerisms. But Chanel, who had a keen admiration for Romy, said: "She is famous before she has even started."
2 A pink suit with a tragic initiation, the Chanel worn by Jaqueline Kennedy on her trip to Dallas in November 1963.

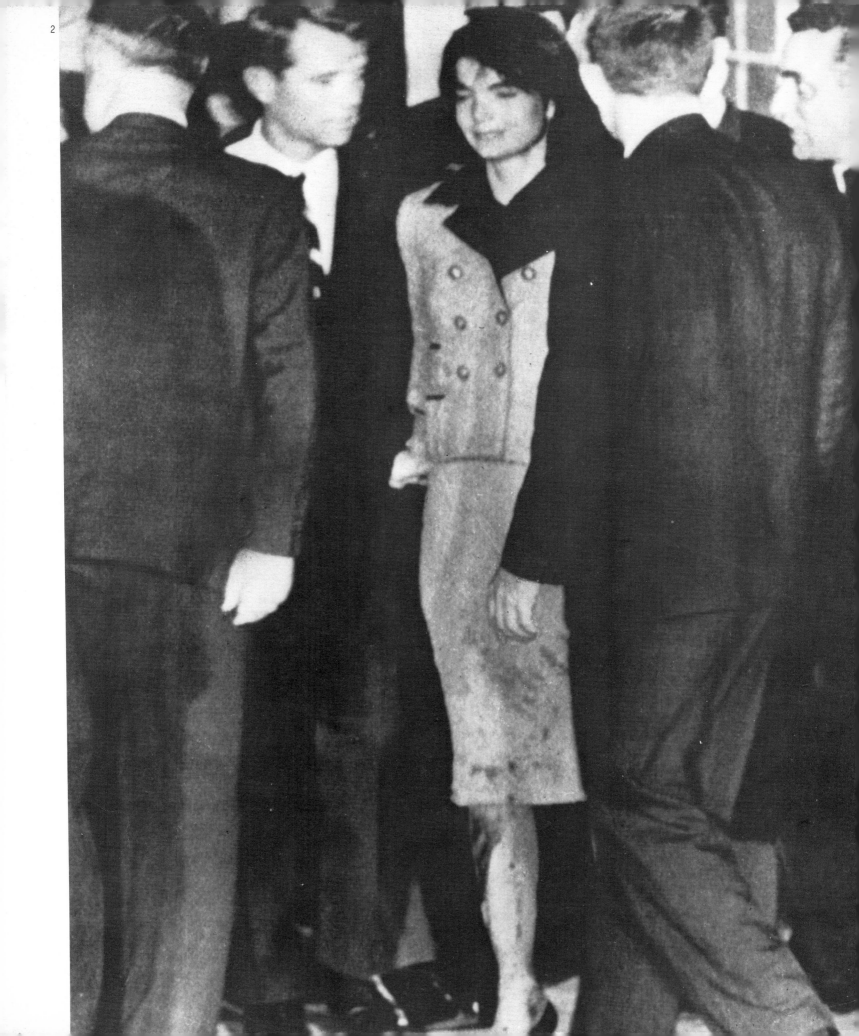

an interior for living

Located at 31 Rue Cambon, right above her boutique and public salons, the private apart- ment of Chanel was photographed by Robert Doisneau around 1954. Altogether, it con- sisted of three rooms whose walls were covered with a simple copper-gold paper, which how- ever was scarcely visible behind lacquered Co- romandel screens, books, and carved wood. As for the eternally traveling screens, those panels always subject to change, it was their obvious movability that created the impression of royal encampment. By the very sumptuous- ness of these assembled pieces, Chanel made evident that she had become the equal of the very rich, but by the sovereign casualness of their placement, without protection of any sort, she managed to indicate that she attached no importance to their monetary value and

at they were there solely for her pleasure.

elow Two successive stages of Chanel's pri-
te salon. At left, a Greek marble dating from
e 5th century B.C. rests on the mantelpiece,
framed, like the mirrors, with sections of
alian Baroque *boiserie*. The Chinese bronze
er date from the 18th century, while the
andirons came from the hand of Jacques Lip-
chitz. On the right, a different kind of framed
mirror, books, and screens. The statue of the
Virgin was made in the 16th century, the
French chair and settee during the Régence
period of the early 18th century. The meteo-
rite came from China, as did the low table in
black lacquer.

consecration by theatre

1970: Chanel on stage, played by Hepburn.

1 Miss Katharine Hepburn in the role of Mademoiselle Chanel. This was big news in the world of New York show biz, for it concerned a musical comedy starring a great actress who had never sung or danced. For years the producer Fred Brisson had been trying to persuade Chanel to let him do a play based on her life, and now she had given her consent. Broadway was to take advantage of the Chanel myth. None other than the *My Fair Lady* team was to prepare the show: Alan Jay Lerner for the lyrics and Sir Cecil Beaton for the 250 costumes. *Coco* became the most expensive production ever to appear on Broadway. Two weeks before opening night, some $1.5 million in tickets had been sold. Despite a poor critical reception, *Coco* played to full houses. Hepburn, who, like Chanel, seemed to defy the passage of time, transcended her 60 years to achieve a personal triumph.

2 Mademoiselle Chanel at home with Alan Jay Lerner and Fred Brisson. She was eighty-seven and would die a year later.

acknowledgments

Among the many debts of gratitude the author has incurred in the course of preparing this book, she wishes most especially to acknowledge those owed to: M. Pierre-Marcel Adéma, Mme Paule d'Alayer, M. Henri Amouroux, the Comte Henri de Beaumont, Mme Sibylle Billot, Sir Cecil Beaton, M. Pierre Bertin, M. Georges Borchardt, Mme Étienne Balsan, the Comtesse Amédée Costa de Beauregard, Mme Marie-Hélène Camus, M. Jean Cardosi, M. David Chierichetti, M. Jérôme Clément, Mme Gabrielle Dorziat, Mme Hélène Dessoffy, Mme Henriette Dussourd, M. Robert Doisneau, Mr. Anton Dolin, M. Frantz Douchnitz, Mme Raymonde Fraisse, M. Benno Graziani, M. Philippe Garner, Mme Georges Gruber-Bernstein, M. Nicolas de Gunzburg, Mme Martine Kahane, M. Boris Kochno, Mrs. Lee Jones, M. Jacques-Henri Lartigue, Mme Gaston Leclere, M. Pierre Lévy, Mr. Marvin Lyons, M. Aimé Maeght, M. Hervé Mille, M. Jean-Yves Mock, M. Ralph Meima, the Vicomte Charles de Noailles, the Baron Ferréol de Nexon, M. Michel Rémy-Bieth, M. André Rossel, M. Antoine Salomon, M. Henri Sauguet, Mme Romy Schneider, Mme Roger Thérond, Mme Denise Tual, Mme Jeanine Warnod, Condé Nast Publications, Inc., Paris and New York.

notes

Page 2
André Breton, *Nadja,* © Gallimard, Paris, 1928.
        , *Point du jour,* © Gallimard, Paris, 1934.
Pages 83, 138, 191, 197
Paul Morand, *L'Allure de Chanel,* © Hermann, Paris, 1976.
Page 116
Misia Sert, *Misia,* © Gallimard, Paris, 1952.
Page 182
Colette, *Prisons et paradis,* Hachette, Paris, 1932.
Page 185
Colette, extract from an unpublished letter to Maurice Goudeket.
Page 186
Paul Morand, *Venises,* © Gallimard, Paris, 1971.

illustrations

Page 4
Musée des Arts et Traditions Populaires, Paris, photo Hyde.
Pages 10–11
1. Photo Hyde, collection Roger Lecotté; 2,3. Photo Rancurel.
Pages 12–13
1–6. Photo Rancurel.
Pages 14–15
1–4. Photo Blanchard, Saumur.
Pages 16–17
1. Photo Simone Brousse, private collection; 2. Photo Blanchard; 3. Hospice de Saumur, photo Decker; 4. Extract from the Saumur birth registry.
Pages 18–19
1,2. Photo CAP, collection Coursaget, published in *Dans les rue de Paris au temps des fiacres* (Édition du Chêne); 3. Atget, Bibliothèque Nationale, Paris; 4. Photo Robert Doisneau/Rapho.
Pages 20–21
1. Photo Ray-Delvert; 2,3. Photo P.H. Martinez; 4. Photo Gonnard; 5,6. Private collection.
Pages 22–23
1. Photo Gonnard, collection Henriette Dussoud; 2. Photo Harlingue-Viollet; 3. Collection Bossi; 4. Photo Gonnard, collection Y. Wendremaire; 5. Bibliothèque Nationale, Paris.
Pages 24–25
1. Collection Jacques Dubois; 2. Photo Rancurel, collection Genermont; 3. Photo Gonnard, collection Charles Coutelard; 4,5. Photo Gonnard, collection Jean-Charles Varennes.
Pages 26–27
1,2. Private collection; 3. Collection Jean-Charles Varennes.
Pages 28–29
1. Collection Genermont; 2. Collection Clément, Archives Départementales de l'Allier.
Pages 30–31
1. Bibliothèque Historique de la Ville de Paris; 2. H.G. Ibels, drawing for *Les Demi-Cabots,* 1906, © SPADEM 1979, Bibliothèque Nationale, Paris; 3. Photo CDRP, Musée Bargouin, Clermont-Ferrand; 4. Collection Pierre Jacquot et Cie.; 5. H.G. Ibels, drawing for *Les Demi-Cabots,* 1906, © SPADEM 1979, Bibliothèque Nationale, Paris; 6. Collection Adrien Eche; 7. Photo CDRP, Musée Bargouin, Clermont-Ferrand; 8. Photo Gonnard, Archives Départementales de l'Allier.
Pages 32–33
1. a.b.c. press, Amsterdam; 2–4. Collection Jean-Charles Varennes.
Pages 34–35
1. Collection Jean-Charles Varennes; 2. Private collection; 3. Bibliothèque de l'Opéra, Paris.
Pages 36–37
1. Private collection; 2. a.b.c. press, Amsterdam.
Pages 38–39
1. Private collection.
Pages 40–41
1. Private collection; 2. Photo DR, Bibliothèque Nationale, Paris; 3. Photo DR, Musée du Costume, Paris.
Pages 42–43
1–3. Private collection.
Pages 44–45
1,2. Private collection.
Pages 46–47
1,3. Collection Société des Steeple Chases de France; 2,4. Photo DR, Bibliothèque Nationale, Paris; 5. Collection Roxane Debuisson.
Pages 48–49
1,2. Collection Sirot-Angel; 3. Collection Marouani; 4. Photo DR, Musée du Costume, Paris; 5. Private collection.
Pages 50–51
1,2. a.b.c. press, Amsterdam; 3. Collection Coursaget; 4. Archives Photographiques, Paris; 5. Centre de Documentation du Costume; 6. Collection Sirot-Angel.
Pages 52–53
1,2. Private collection.
Pages 54–55
1. Collection Viollet; 2,3. Private collection; 4. Archives Photographiques, Paris.
Pages 56–57
1,4,6. Private collection; 2,3,5. *Studio Vogue France.*
Pages 58–59
1,4,7. Private collection; 2,3,5,6. *Studio Vogue,* France.
Pages 60–61
1. Collection Seeberger, Bibliothèque Nationale, Paris; 2. Collection Sirot-Angel; 3,4. Private collection.
Pages 62–63
1,2. Private collection.
pages 64–65
1,2. *Vogue Studio* London; 3. a.b.c. press, Amsterdam; 4. Private collection.
Pages 66–67
Private collection.
Pages 68–69
1,2. Private collection.
Pages 70–71
1,2. Photo DR, published in *Comoedia,* 1912, Bibliothèque Nationale, Paris.
Pages 72–73
1. Photo DR, published in *Les Modes,* 1912, Bibliothèque Nationale, Paris; 2. Photo DR, published in *Comoedia,* 1912, Bibliothèque Nationale, Paris; 3. Photo Keystone; 4. Photo Henri Manuel, published in *Comoedia,* c. 1913; 5. Photo de Boissonas, private collection; 6. Photo Henri Manuel, published in *Comoedia,* 1913; 7. Worth, drawing by Cappiello, © SPADEM 1979, published in *Les Années folles* (Guilleminault, Denoël, 1958); 8. Collection Sirot-Angel; 9. Doucet, drawing by Capiello, © SPADEM 1979, published in *Les Modes,* 1912, photo DR, Bibliothèque Nationale, Paris; 10. Photo Seeberger, Bibliothèque Nationale, Paris; 11. Poiret, drawing by Oberlé, published in *Les Années folles* (Guilleminault, Denoël, 1958); 12. Photo Seeberger, Bibliothèque Nationale, Paris.
Pages 74–75
1. Photo Keystone; 2. Photo DR, published in *Les Modes,* 1912, Bibliothèque Nationale, Paris.
Pages 76–77
1. Photo Seeberger, Bibliothèque Nationale, Paris; 2,3. Private collection.
Pages 78–79
1–4,6. Collection Marcel Jouhandeau; 5. Collection Michel Rémy-Bieth.
Pages 80–81
1. Miró, *Nord-Sud,* 1917, © ADAGP 1979, photo Galerie Maeght; 2. Picasso, *Portrait de Pierre Reverdy,* 1921, © SPADEM 1979, collection Fondation Maeght, photo Claude Gaspari; 3. Collection Pierrette Gargallo.
Pages 82–83
1,2. Collection Sirot-Angel; 3,4. Private collection.
Pages 84–85
1. a.b.c. press, Amsterdam; 2. Collection Chennebenoist; 3. Private collection.
Pages 86–87
1,2. Private collection.
Pages 88–89
1,2. Drawings by Sem, © SPADEM 1979.
Pages 90–91
1. *Coco Chanel et Boy Capel,* drawing by Sem, © SPADEM 1979; 2. Collection Chennebenoist; 3. Drawing by Sem, © SPADEM 1979.
Pages 92–93
1,2. a.b.c. press, Amsterdam.
Pages 94–95
1. Collection Chennebenoist; 2. Private collection; 3. Private collection:
Pages 96–97
1. Collection Sirot-Angel; 2. Photo AFP.
Pages 98–99
1. Photo Marie-Claire; 2. Collection Sirot-Angel; 3. Photo published in *Harper's Bazaar,* © Hearst Corp.
Pages 100–101
1. Private collection; 2. Photo DR; 3,4. Drawings published in *Les Élégances parisiennes,* 1917; 5. Photo Harry B. Lachman, published in *Fémina,* 1917.
Pages 102–103
1,2. Private collection; 3. Photo published in *Fémina,* 1917; 4,5. Private collection.
Pages 104–105
1–4. Private collection.
Pages 106–107
1. Photo Talbot, published in *Comoedia;* 2. Photo DR, Bibliothèque de l'Opéra; 3. Private collection; 4. Amedeo Modigliani, *Portrait de Madame Kisling,* © ADAGP 1979, photo Musées Nationaux, Paris; 5. Collection Marcel Jouhandeau.
Pages 108–109
1,2. Private collection.
Pages 110–111
1–3. Private collection.
Pages 112–113
1. Édouard Vuillard, *Misia Sert,* 1897, © SPADEM 1979, private collection; 2. Vuillard, *Misia,* 1896, © SPADEM 1979, private collection.
Pages 114–115
1. Collection Boris Kochno; 2. Pierre Bonnard, poster for *La Revue blanche,* 1894, © SPADEM 1979; 3. Henri de Toulouse-Lautrec, poster for *La Revue blanche,* 1895, © SPADEM 1979.
Pages 116–117
1. Pierre Bonnard, *Portrait de Misia,* 1908–09, © SPADEM and ADAGP 1979, collection Mrs. J. Neff; 2. Collection Boris Kochno.
Pages 118–119
1. Édouard Vuillard, *Misia,* 1915, © SPADEM 1979, private collection; 2. Jean Cocteau, *Misia Sert aux Ballets russes lors de la création du Spectre de la Rose,* 1911, © SPADEM 1979, Bibliothèque de l'Opéra (collection Boris Kochno), Paris.
Page 120
1. Collection Boris Kochno.
Page 121
1. Roger de la Fresnaye, *Raymond Radiguet,* Bibliothèque Doucet, Paris, © SPADEM 1979; 2,3. Collection Michel Rémy-Bieth; 4. Oberlé, drawing.
Pages 122–123
1. Collection Benoîte Groult; 2. Collection Henri de Beaumont; 3. Picasso, *Portrait d'Etienne de Beaumont,* © SPADEM 1979, private collection.
Pages 124–125
1. Private collection; 2. Collection Georges Gruber-Bernstein.
Pages 126–127
1. Private collection; 2. Collection Marvin Lyons; 3,4. Private collection; 5. A.E. Marty, drawing published in *Vogue,* Paris, 1921, © SPADEM 1979; 6. Photo DR; 7. Collection Marvin Lyons.
Pages 128–129
1. Collection Georges Gruber-Bernstein; 2. Drawing published in *Vogue,* Paris, 1923, © Vogue France; 3. Photo *Saturday Evening Post;* 4. Olga Thomas, drawing published in *Vogue,* Paris, 1920, © Vogue France; 5. Private collection; 6. Mario de Goyon, *Portrait of Marthe Davelli,* published in *Vogue,* Paris, 1920; 7,9,10,12. Drawings published in *Vogue,* Paris, © Vogue France; 8. Photo Seeberger, Bibliothèque Nationale, Paris; 11. Photo Pratin Lévy, private collection.
Pages 130–131
1. Photo published in *Match,* November 4, 1967; 2. Olga Thomas, drawing published in *Vogue,* March 1, 1920, © Vogue France; 3. Private collection; 4. Reynaldo Luza, drawing published in *Vogue,* Paris, 1922, © Vogue France; 5. Collection Marvin Lyons; 6. Drawing published in *Vogue,* Paris, 1922, © Vogue France; 7. Woodruff, drawing published in *Vogue,* Paris, 1923, © Vogue France; 8. Collection Marvin Lyons (detail of photo on page 169); 9. Drawing published in *Vogue,* Paris, 1923, © Vogue France.
Pages 132–133
Photo Talpain.
Pages 134–135
1. Photo Wladimir Rehbinder, published in *Rheinische Blätter,* March 1923; 2. Lepape, drawing, © SPADEM 1979, published in *Vogue,* Paris, February 1923.
Pages 136–137
1–4. Private collection.
Pages 138–139
1. Drian, drawing, © ADAGP 1979 and the Hearst Corp., published in *Harper's Bazaar;* 3. Drawing published in *Vogue,* Paris, 1924, © Vogue France; 4. Collection Sirot-Angel; 2,5,6. Bibliothèque de l'Opéra (collection Boris Kochno), Paris; 7. Drawing published in *Vogue,* Paris, January 1924, © Vogue France; 8. Photo ADP, *Le Provençal* archives; 9. Drawing published in *Vogue,* Paris, January 1924, © Vogue France.
Pages 140–141
1. Kees Van Dongen, drawing for the cover of Victor Margueritte's *La Garçonne,* © SPADEM 1979; 2. Collection Georges Gruber-Bernstein; 3. Berings, drawing published in *L'Illustration,* Paris; 4. Drawing published in Rossana Bussageio's *Il Deco italiano* (Rizzoli); 5,6. Private collection; 7. Berings, drawing published in *L'Illustration,* Paris; 8. Collection Georges Gruber-Bernstein; 9. Collection Sirot-Angel; 10,11. Collection Père Rzewuski; 12. Collection Boris Kochno.
Pages 142–143
1. Photo Keystone; 2. Bibliothèque de l'Opéra, Paris. 3. Picasso, drawings for the

Ballets Russes program, 1924, © SPADEM 1979, Bibliothèque de l'Opéra, Paris.
4. Collection Anton Dolin.
Pages 144–145
1. Photo Sasha, collection Anton Dolin, London; **2.** Photo J.-H. Lartigue; **3.** Bibliothèque de l'Opéra (collection Boris Kochno), Paris; **4.** Photo J.-H. Lartigue; **5.** Bibliothèque de l'Opéra (collection Boris Kochno), Paris.
Pages 146–147
1. Collection Laurens, photo published in *Henri Laurens* (Ministère d'État des Affaires Culturelles), 1967; **2,3.** Photo *The Times,* London.
Pages 148–149
1. Picasso, *La Course,* Theater Museum, Victoria and Albert Museum, London, © SPADEM 1979.
Pages 150–151
1. Photo Édition du Chêne, by courtesy of the Theater Museum, London; **2.** Collection Amédée Costa de Beauregard; **3.** Collection Henri de Beaumont; **4.** Collection Amédée Costa de Beauregard.
Pages 152–153
1. Photo Horst; **2.** Boucher, drawing published in *Vogue,* Paris, 1925, © Vogue France.
Pages 154–155
1. Kees Van Dongen, drawing for the cover of Paul Morand's *Magie noire* (Grasset, Paris), © SPADEM 1979; **2.** Académie Française archives (Morand fund).
Pages 156–157
1. Drawing, published in *Vogue,* Paris, 1926, © Vogue France; **2.** Drawing, published in *Vogue,* Paris, January 1927, © Vogue France; **3.** Drawing, published in *Vogue,* Paris, January 1927, © Vogue France.
Pages 158–159
Douglas Polland, drawings published in *Vogue,* Paris, January 1927, © Vogue France.
Pages 160–161
Photo Robert Doisneau/Rapho.
Pages 162–163
1. Radio Times Hulton Picture Library, London; **2.** Collection Chanel-Lajet; **3.** Collection Henri de Beaumont; **4.** Collection Chanel-Lajet.
Pages 164–165
1. Photo *Sunday Telegraph;* **2.** Private collection.
Pages 166–167
1. *L'Illustration* archives; **2.** Drawing published in *Vogue,* Paris, 1927, © Vogue France; **3.** Photo Keystone; **4.** Private collection.
Pages 168–169
1. Photo Seeberger, Bibliothèque Nationale, Paris; **2.** Collection Boris Kochno; **3.** Photo *Sunday Telegraph;* **4.** Photo Roger Schall.
Pages 170–171
1,2. Collection Sacha Pitoëff; **3.** Collection Amédée Costa de Beauregard.
Pages 172–173
1,2. Collection Henri de Beaumont; **3.** Bibliothèque Nationale, Paris.
Pages 174–175
1. Photo Jean Roubier; **2.** Cocteau, drawing published in *Chanel en 1938,* © SPADEM 1979, collection Galerie Proscenium; **3.** Cocteau, drawing published in

Chanel en 1932, © SPADEM 1979, collection Galerie Proscenium.
Pages 176–177
1,2. Cinémathèque Française; **3,4.** Collection Cecil B. De Mille Trust.
Pages 178–179
Cinémathèque Française.
Pages 180–181
1,3,4,5. *L'Illustration* archives; **2.** J.-G. Domergue, painting published in *L'Illustration,* Paris, © SPADEM 1979, photo *L'Illustration* archives.
Pages 182–183
Private collection.
Pages 184–185
1. Photo J.-H. Lartigue; **2.** Private collection; **3.** Collection Leclère.
Pages 186–187
1. Drawing published in *Vogue,* Paris, 1927, © Vogue France; **2.** Collection Boris Kochno.
Pages 188–189
1. *Match* archives; **2.** Collection The Museum of Modern Art (Film Stills Archive), New York.
Pages 190–191
Collection Henri de Beaumont.
Pages 192–193
1,2. Collection Denise Tual; **3.** Private collection.
Pages 194–195
1. Drawing published in *Vogue,* Paris, June 1929; **2–6.** Collection Henri de Beaumont.
Pages 196–197
1. Drawing published in *Vogue,* Paris, 1929, © Vogue France; **2,3.** Drawing published in *Vogue,* Paris, November 1931, © Vogue France.
Pages 198–199
1. Drawing published in *Vogue,* Paris, February 1930, © Vogue France; **2,3.** Drian, drawings, Paris, 1921, 1931, Collection Seeberger, Bibliothèque Nationale, Paris; **4.** Photo Horst P. Horst, © Horst.
Pages 200–201
1. Steichen, photo published in *Vogue,* New York, April 1930, © Condé Nast Publications, Inc., New York; **2.** Cecil Beaton, photo published in *Vogue,* New York, December 1935, © Condé Nast Publications, Inc., New York.
Pages 202–203
1. Private collection; **2,3.** Paul Iribe, drawing for *Le Témoin,* © SPADEM 1979, private collection.
Pages 204–205
1,3. Photo Lipnitzki-Viollet; **2.** Collection Pierre Jacquot et Cie.
Pages 206–207
1,3. Photo Roger Schall; **2.** Bibliothèque Nationale, Paris, photo Édition du Chêne.
Pages 208–209
1,2. Collection Visconti; **3.** Photo Bibliothèque Nationale, Paris.
Pages 212–213
1,3. Photo Lipnitzki-Viollet; **2.** Jean Cocteau, drawing, 1937, © SPADEM 1979, collection Dermit.
Pages 214–215
Photo Horst P. Horst, 1936, © Horst.
Pages 216–217
1. Christian Bérard, drawing published in *Vogue,* Paris, 1936 and 1937, © SPADEM 1979; **2–4.** Photo Roger Schall.
Pages 218–219
1. Photo Hoyningen-Huene, ©

Horst; **2,3.** Photo Cecil Beaton, © Condé Nast Publications, Inc., New York.
Pages 220–221
1–5. Photo Roger Schall.
Pages 222–223
1. Christian Bérard, drawing published in *Vogue,* Paris, 1937, © SPADEM 1979; **2.** Boucher, drawing published in *Vogue,* Paris, 1938, © Vogue France; **3.** Pagès, drawing published in *Vogue,* Paris, 1938, © Vogue France; **4.** Eric, drawing published in *Vogue,* Paris, 1939, © Vogue France.
Pages 224–225
1–3, 5–14. Photo Roger Schall; **4.** Private collection.
Pages 226–227
Photo Richard Avedon.
Pages 228–229
1. Christian Bérard, drawing published in *Vogue,* © SPADEM 1979; **2.** Dior archives.
Pages 230–231
Photo Robert Doisneau/Rapho.
Pages 232–233
1. Drawing published in *Vogue,* Paris, 1954, © Vogue France; **2.** Photo J.F. Clair/Elle-Scoop.
Pages 234–235
1. Irving Penn, photo published in *Vogue,* New York, © Condé Nast Publications, Inc., New York (negative Studio Vogue); **2,3.** Photo Frances MacLaughlin.
Pages 236–237
Photo Hatami.
Pages 238–239
Photo Hatami.
Pages 240–241
Photo Hatami.
Pages 242–243
Photo Hatami.
Pages 244–245
1. Photo Hatami; **2.** Photo United Press.
Pages 246–247
Photo Robert Doisneau/Rapho.
Pages 248–249
1. Cecil Beaton, photo published in *Vogue,* © Condé Nast Publications, Inc., New York; **2,3.** Photo Hatami.
Pages 250–251
Photo Hatami.

index

who was who in the world of Chanel

Chanel's world was one in which "names" could be dropped with the sure assumption that they would have instant recognition. To help English-language readers with this aspect of the Parisian *monde* in the first half of the 20th century, the following biographical notes have been prepared. They briefly identify figures who had to be mentioned in the Chanel story but whose involvement with the great *couturière* did not warrant the full development given such intimates as Étienne Balsan, Arthur Capel, Misia Sert, Pierre Reverdy, Jean Cocteau, Bend'or, Duke of Westminster, and Paul Iribe. Needless to say, no entries have been made for the likes of Picasso, Diaghilev, Stravinsky, Churchill, or de Gaulle, historic personalities as universally familiar today as in Chanel's time.

Apollinaire, Guillaume (1880–1918)
French poet and critic born in Rome of Polish parents. Became a vigorous defender of the avant-garde, from Cubism through Dada. The first to use the word "surrealism" in print. His *Alcools* (1913) and *Calligrammes* (1918) must be counted among the key works of modernism. Died of head wounds suffered during World War I.

Aragon, Louis (1887–   )
Poet, novelist, and essayist with a long and extensive involvement with the French avant-garde. Active in both the Surrealist movement and the Communist Party.

Artaud, Antonin (1896–1948)
An actor, a leading avant-gardist in French theatre, and the author of two manifestoes presenting his theory of a theatre of cruelty. Artaud suffered period mental breakdowns and public indifference, but has now been recognized as a forerunner of the Living Theatre.

Auric, Georges (1899–   )
Founder, along with Milhaud, Honegger, Poulenc, etc., of Les Six, a group of anti-Wagner, anti-Debussy, but modernist French composers. Wrote the music for *Les Fâcheux*, a ballet produced by Diaghilev in the 1920s.

Bakst, Léon (1866–1926)
After an early involvement with Imperial Russia's "World of Art" movement, whose purpose was to introduce Russians to the most advanced ideas in Western art and culture, Bakst later became associated with Diaghilev. As the principal set and costume designer to the Ballets Russes, he gained international fame, especially for the rich exoticism of his taste.

Barrès, Maurice (1862–1923)
French writer and politician offering a powerful advocacy of personal independence, which evolved into a pronounced form of nationalism and traditionalism. Key spokesman for France's reacquisition of Alsace-Lorrain after World War I.

Bataille, Henry (1872–1922)
French playwright long popular on the Parisian boulevards. Specialized in plays dealing with contemporary manners and morals, their impact based more on intrigue than on character development.

Baur, Harry (1880–1943)
Popular French actor who played Jean Valjean in *Les Misérables* (1934), the inspector in *Crime and Punishment* (1936), and the title role in *Volpone* (1939), all major French films of the period.

Bérard, Christian (1902–49)
A painter associated with the Neo-Romanticism that also claimed Eugène Berman and Pavel Tchelitchew (a movement whose mystery and fantasy came from Surrealism but whose aim was to react against both Cubist abstraction and Surrealism), Bérard figured large in the world of Chanel, mainly through his activity as a stage designer for both theatre and ballet. He may be best known for his work on the sets and costumes for Cocteau's *La Voix humaine, La Machine infernale, Les Parents terribles,* and *La Belle et la bête,* as well as for Giraudoux's *Madwoman of Chaillot.*

Bernstein, Henri (1876–1953)
One of the most successful French playwrights of his time, Bernstein was no less triumphant in conversation, love, and physical courage—the latter characteristic tempting him into a duel when he was well past fifty.

Berthelot, Philippe (1866–1934)
A key formulator and administrator of French foreign policy in the period before, during, and after World War I. Closely associated with Clémenceau and the official under whom Paul Morand, Chanel's close friend, worked at the Ministère des Affaires Étrangères.

Blum, Léon (1872–1950)
Born of a wealthy and cultivated Alsatian Jewish family, Blum began his career as a brilliant intellectual, a sensitive aesthete, a seductive conversationalist, and the author of a book on love. In middle age, he turned to politics, joined the French Socialist Party, and founded the newspaper *Le Populaire.* In 1936, as leader of the Front Populaire, a leftist coalition, he became France's first Socialist Prime Minister and instituted many important political and social changes.

Bourget, Paul (1852–1935)
Author of important essays on the psychology of contemporary Europe, but best known for his many novels, all of a strong psychological and moral cast.

Castellane, Comte Boni de (1867–1932)
A great dandy of the Belle Époque, Boni de Castellane married the American railroad heiress Anna Gould and became one of the famed hosts of the period, entertaining lavishly at the Palais de Marbre Rose in Paris and at Le Marais, a sumptuous 18th-century château on the Seine northwest of Paris. He also served as the model for one of Proust's main characters.

Claudel, Paul (1868–1955)
French diplomat and one of the greatest French poets of all time. Claudel's verse plays are all highly symbolic and imbued with deeply religious, Catholic feeling.

Daladier, Édouard (1884–1970)
French radical Socialist politician and professor of history. In the 1930s a leading promoter of the Front Populaire. A pacifist, Daladier signed the Munich Accord in 1938 on behalf of France, but a year later, as Head of State, he declared war on a belligerent Germany. He then ceded the top position to Paul Reynaud and became Minister of War. Interned by the Vichy government and deported to Germany during the Occupation.

Doucet, Jacques (1853–1929)
Art collector and writer on art, but best known as one of the great Parisian *couturiers* of the Belle Époque.

Dullin, Charles (1885–1949)
Actor, producer, and, as founder of the Vieux Colombier, a significant force in French theatre from 1913 until his death.

Fellowes, The Hon. Mrs. Reginald
Born of a French-Danish Duke and an American mother (*née* Singer), then first married to Prince Jean de Broglie, "Daisy" Fellowes, with her beauty, taste, wealth, and originality, became one of the great *locomotives* of the Parisian *haut monde* in the 1930s. At her house in Neuilly she entertained lavishly right up to the outbreak of World War II.

Fénéon, Félix (1861–1944)
Writer, critic, and key apologist for the avant-garde during the Symbolist period at the end of the 19th century. With Verlaine and Mallarmé, Fénéon edited *La Revue indépendante,* and with Thadée Natanson, *La Revue blanche* (1893–1905).

Foch, Ferdinand (1851–1929)
Marshal of France and his nation's great military hero of World War I.

Flanner, Janet (1892–1978)
American born and bred, Parisian by choice and adoption, Flanner first went to live in France in 1922 and became Paris correspondent for *The New Yorker* when it was founded in 1925. Her letters from Paris, signed Genêt, were one of the magazine's most distinguished regular features for almost half a century.

Garros, Roland (1888–1918)
An ace fighter-pilot entrusted with the defense of Paris during World War I. His charm seduced Cocteau and many others of the contemporary Parisian *monde.* After a two-year imprisonment by the Germans, Garros returned to battle, only to be killed on his third mission. Cocteau's *Le Cap de Bonne-Espérance,* a cycle of poems, was written as a memorial tribute to the dead hero.

Goncharova, Natalia (1881–1962)
A leading member of the Russian avant-garde who, with her husband Mikhail Larionov, started a movement called Rayonnism (1912–13), a Futurist-like offshoot of Cubism that sought to give visual expression to the new mathematical concepts of time and space. Larionov and Goncharova both left Russia after the Revolution and settled in Paris, there becoming important figures in the world of art and theatre. Goncharova also worked in a folkloric manner, especially in the ballets she designed for Diaghilev—*Les Noces* and *Firebird.*

Guilbert, Yvette (1867–1944)
French music-hall performer and probably the greatest of her day. A favorite subject of Toulouse-Lautrec.

Guitry, Sacha (1885–1957)
France's quintessential boulevard playwright and actor throughout an incredibly long and prolific career.

Gunzburg, Baron Nicholas de
The son of a Russian father and a Polish-Brazilian mother, Baron Nicholas de Gunzburg was educated in England but made his mark in the Parisian *monde* of the 1920s and 30s as a young man of elegance, distinguished taste, and dark good looks. In 1934 he, along with his close friends Prince and Princesse Jean-Louis de Faucigny-Lucinge, gave one of prewar Paris' most memorable fancy-dress balls—*Le Bal des valses.* Shortly thereafter he left France for the USA, where he was long associated with the New York fashion industry.

Honegger, Arthur (1892–1955)
Swiss-born composer who studied under France's Vidor and d'Indy and joined with Milhaud, Poulenc, Auric, Tailleferre, etc., to form Les Six, a group of modernist, polytonal composers interested in integrating the classical tradition with such popular sources as folk music and "café-concert." Frequently set the verses of Apollinaire, Cocteau, Claudel, and Giraudoux.

Jacob, Max (1876–1944)
A poet and intimate of the Parisian avant-garde, Jacob joined with Apollinaire to found *Les Soirées de Paris,* a magazine designed to celebrate the emergence of Fauvism, Cubism, and Futurism. Sensual and puritan, witty and mystical, a Jew and a convert to Catholicism (with Picasso as his godfather), Jacob went to live at the Abbey of Saint Benoît-sur-Loire in the 1930s, where he was seized in February, 1944. Despite the efforts of Cocteau, Utrillo, Braque, Picasso, Sacha Guitry, and José-Maria Sert, Max Jacob perished in a Nazi concentration camp shortly before the end of World War II.

Jammes, Francis (1868–1938)
French poet and novelist deeply imbued with Catholic mysticism. Carried on a rich correspondence with such figures as Colette and Gide.

Jarry, Alfred (1873–1938)
Famous for his *naïf,* cynical, and mystical play *Ubu roi* (1888), written when the author was still a teenager and produced in 1896 by the Théâtre de l'Oeuvre. Invented "pataphysique," a new so-called science. Jarry much admired by the Dadaists.

Jouvet, Louis (1887–1958)
Actor, stage manager, director, producer, and teacher, Jouvet all but dominated French theatre for some four decades, ending only in 1950. He began with Jacques Copeau's company at the Vieux Colombier, but subsequently went on to become associated with such brilliant productions as Jules Romains' *Knock,* Giraudoux's *Amphitryon 38,* and Cocteau's *La Machine infernal,* Molière's *L'École des femmes,* Giraudoux's *La Guerre de Troie n'aura pas lieu, Ondine,* and *The Madwoman of Chaillot.* He also supervised productions at the Comédie-Française and taught as Professor at the Paris Conservatoire.

Kessel, Joseph (1898–1979)
French writer and journalist who first gained attention for his romantic accounts of early exploits in aviation. Realized a long and prolific career writing for the *Journal des débats, Le Matin, Le Figaro, Paris-Soir,* and *France-Soir.* Became an authority on Russia.

Kochno, Boris (1905–   )
From 1922 private secretary to Sergei de Diaghilev. Also prepared librettos for many of the ballets created by the Ballets Russes. Later with the Monte Carlo Ballet. In the 1930s Kochno collaborated with Balanchine, and in 1945 he joined with Christian Bérard to direct the Ballets des Champs-Élysées.

La Gandara, Antonio de (1862–1917)
French painter known for his society portraits and his views of the Luxembourg Gardens.

Lanoux, Armand (1913–   )
French man of letters with a special interest in art and television.

Lartigue, Jacques (1894–   )
Began as a painter but became one of the foremost photographers of his time.

Laval, Pierre (1883–1945)
France's Socialist-pacifist politician in charge of the Foreign Ministry in the 1930s and the person largely responsible for his nation's appeasement of Fascist Italy and Nazi Germany. Under Pétain, during the Occupation, Laval became Minister of State at Vichy. Executed as a traitor in 1945.

Leclerc, Philippe Marie de Hautecloc-que (1902–1946)
French military leader who served brilliantly on the Marne during World War I. After France's surrender in 1940, joined de Gaulle in London. In 1944 he became the liberator of Paris.

Marais, Jean (1912–   )
Discovered by Cocteau, Marais achieved his first success as the youthful hero of the poet's *Les Parents terribles* (1937). After election to the Comédie-Française in 1941, Marais went on to star in Cocteau's *L'Éternal retour* (1943), *La Belle et la bête* (1945), and *Orphée* (1950). His career in France has been equally distinguished on stage and screen.

Maurras, Charles (1868–1952)
French writer and politician from Provence. A great advocate of classicism, order, and reason, ideas that the author expressed in nationalistic and traditionalist terms. Considerably influenced by Barrès. A conservative bourgeois, Maurras supported Pétain after 1940.

Milhaud, Darius (1892–1974)
French modernist composer who joined with Honegger, Poulenc, Auric, Tailleferre, etc., to form Le Groupe des Six. Provided the music for *Le Boeuf sur le toit* and *Le Train bleu*, two of the most famous ballets produced by Diaghilev's Ballets Russes during the 1920s.

Mirbeau, Octave (1848–1917)
A writer and violent critic of contemporary French society, first from a royalist perspective and then from that of an anarchist.

Mistinguett (1875–1956)
For generations a seemingly ageless and indestructible institution, "La Miss" made her debut as a music-hall performer in the early part of the 20th century and in 1925 reached the summit, performing at Paris' Moulin Rouge. She starred again and again at the Casino de Paris and the Folies-Bergère. Her closest associate, both on stage and off, was Maurice Chevalier, who, to account for Mistinguett's enduring appeal, wrote: *C'était Paris, ça!*

Morand, Paul (1888–1976)
Diplomat and writer who, during the teens, twenties, and thirties, served France in London, Rome, Madrid, and Thailand, all the while producing one book after another (both fiction and fact), written for the most part with the impressionistic and stream-of-consciousness techniques characteristic of modernism. Among his titles are *Londres, New York, Le Flagéllant de Séville, Lewis et Irène, Magie noire, L'Allure de Chanel, Venise,* and *Journal d'un attaché d'ambassade.* After service in Bucharest and Berne during the German occupation of France, Morand held no further appointments abroad and took official retirement in 1950.

Moréno, Marguerite (1871–1948)
One of the great and enduring actresses of the modern French stage, who worked at the Comédie-Française, with Sarah Bernhardt, and in some 70 films. Created the principal female role in Colette's *Chéri* and Giraudoux's *Madwoman of Chaillot.* Had many close relationships among writers—Mallarmé, Verlaine, Colette. Her fifty-year correspondence with the latter has now been published.

Noailles, Vicomtesse de Marie-Laure
Daughter of the banker Bischoffsheim, granddaughter of Proust's *inspiratrice,* Mme de Chévigné, and a descendant of the Marquis de Sade, Marie-Laure de Noailles married the younger son of the holder of one of the most illustrious ducal titles in France. She was also a poet and painter and a prominent patroness of the Paris literary, artistic, and political avant-garde in the 1930s. The Noailles supported Cocteau and became the principal backers of Buñuel and Dalí's *Le Chien andalou* (1928), Buñuel's *L'Age d'or* (1930), and Cocteau's *Le Sang d'un poète* (1931). The Vicomtesse remained a friend of modern artists and musicians, among them the American composer Ned Rorem, until her death.

Pitoëff, Ludmilla (1896–1951)
Like her husband, Georges Pitoëff, born in Tiflis, Russia, but worked mainly in France. A major actress of the French stage throughout the twenties and thirties.

Pitoëff, Georges (1884–1939)
Born in Tiflis, Russia, but realized a long, prolific, and genuinely brilliant career in the French theatre. A disciple of Stanislavsky and Meyerhold, Pitoëff and his actress wife staged some 200 plays in Paris—Chekhov, Pirandello, Shaw, Gorky, O'Neill, Claudel, Tolstoy, Strindberg, etc.—eschewing Symbolism, Impressionism, and Naturalism to present the works with clarity and directness.

Polaire (1877–1939)
Great star of French music hall and long associated with Willy and Colette. Played Claudine in an operetta production of Colette's *Claudine à l'ècole.*

Poulenc, Francis (1899–1963)
Founding member of Les Six (Honegger, Auric, Milhaud, Tailleferre, etc.), the group of modernist French composers. In his melodic and personal vein he wrote *Les Mamelles de Tirésias,* and in his deeply humane, religious vein, *La Dialogue des carmélites.*

Reynaud, Paul (1878–1966)
French rightist, Republican politician who was hostile to the Front Populaire of the 1930s. Succeeded Daladier as Head of State at the height of the crisis in 1940. Made Pétain Vice President of the Conseil d'État, which led to the government at Vichy. Deported to Germany during the Occupation.

Roussel, Raymond (1877–1933)
Born into a rich bourgeois family, a writer whose extraordinary imagination produced such shifts in form and sense that he came to appeal not only to the Surrealists but also to the later Structuralists (Butor and Robbe-Grillet, for example).

Thorez, Maurice (1900–1964)
An eloquent coalminer from northeastern France, Thorez throughout the thirties and even thereafter was the leading spokesman for French Communists. He won a seat in the Chamber of Deputies in 1936.

Vallotton, Félix (1900–1964)
Swiss-born painter closely allied to the Nabis group headed by Bonnard, Vuillard, Denis, etc. Style much affected by Japanese prints, with all their patterned flatness, brilliant color, and strong graphic effects. Often bitter and acerbic in mood.

Weygand, Maxime (1867–1965)
French General and *chef d'état major* under Foch in World War I. Recalled in 1939 to replace the ineffectual Gamelin. Became Minister of Defense at Vichy, but arrested and deported to Germany during the Occupation.

Willy (1859–1931)
Born Henry Gauthier-Villars but known by the pseudonym given above. His prolific output of novels, plays, and criticism was made possible by a stable of hired writers whose works he signed as his own, among them the first efforts of his young wife, the great Colette. Along with humor, he also published somewhat salacious material.

Worth, Charles Frédéric (1825–95)
An Englishman who became France's greatest *couturier* in the 19th century. Created the elaborate fashions favored by the Empress Eugénie.